Com
NEW JERSEY
BIRDS

Paul E. Lehman, Krista Kagume
& Gregory Kennedy

Lone Pine Publishing International

The Distributor: Lone Pine Publishing
1808 B Street NW, Suite 140
Auburn, WA, USA 98001

Website: www.lonepinepublishing.com

Library and Archives Canada Cataloguing in Publication

Lehman, Paul, 1956-

  Compact guide to New Jersey birds / Paul Lehman, Krista
Kagume, Gregory Kennedy.

Includes bibliographical references and index.
ISBN-13: 978-976-8200-24-2

  1. Birds—New Jersey—Identification. 2. Bird watching—New
Jersey. I. Kennedy, Gregory, 1956- II. Kagume, Krista III. Title.

QL684.N5L44 2007   598.09749   C2006-903713-2

Illustrations: Gary Ross, Ted Nordhagen, Ewa Pluciennik
Digital Scanning: Elite Lithographers Co.
Egg Photography: Alan, Biddy, Gary Whyte

We wish to thank the Royal Alberta Museum for providing access to
their egg collections.

PC: P1

Contents

Snow Goose
size 32 in • p. 20

Canada Goose
size 42 in • p. 22

Mute Swan
size 60 in • p. 24

Wood Duck
size 17 in • p. 26

Gadwall
size 20 in • p. 28

American Black Duck
size 22 in • p. 30

Mallard
size 24 in • p. 32

Green-winged Teal
size 14 in • p. 34

Greater Scaup
size 18 in • p. 36

Surf Scoter
size 19 in • p. 38

Black Scoter
size 19 in • p. 40

Long-tailed Duck
size 19 in • p. 42

Common Merganser
size 25 in • p. 44

Wild Turkey
size 39 in • p. 46

Common Loon
size 31 in • p. 48

Horned Grebe
size 14 in • p. 50

Northern Gannet
size 38 in • p. 52

Double-crested Cormorant
size 29 in • p. 54

WATERFOWL

TURKEYS

DIVING BIRDS

Great Blue Heron
size 51 in • p. 56

Great Egret
size 39 in • p. 58

Snowy Egret
size 24 in • p. 60

Green Heron
size 18 in • p. 62

Glossy Ibis
size 24 in • p. 64

Turkey Vulture
size 28 in • p. 66

Osprey
size 23 in • p. 68

Northern Harrier
size 20 in • p. 70

Sharp-shinned Hawk
size 12 in • p. 72

Cooper's Hawk
size 17 in • p. 74

Broad-winged Hawk
size 17 in • p. 76

Red-tailed Hawk
size 23 in • p. 78

American Kestrel
size 8 in • p. 80

Clapper Rail
size 14 in • p. 82

American Coot
size 14 in • p. 84

Black-bellied Plover
size 12 in • p. 86

Killdeer
size 10 in • p. 88

American Oystercatcher
size 18 in • p. 90

Greater Yellowlegs
size 14 in • p. 92

Willet
size 15 in • p. 94

Sanderling
size 8 in • p. 96

Least Sandpiper
size 6 in • p. 98

Purple Sandpiper
size 9 in • p. 100

Laughing Gull
size 16 in • p. 102

Ring-billed Gull
size 19 in • p. 104

Herring Gull
size 24 in • p. 106

Great Black-backed Gull
size 30 in • p. 108

Common Tern
size 15 in • p. 110

Rock Pigeon
size 12 in • p. 112

Mourning Dove
size 12 in • p. 114

Yellow-billed Cuckoo
size 12 in • p. 116

Eastern Screech-Owl
size 8 in • p. 118

Great Horned Owl
size 21 in • p. 120

Chimney Swift
size 5 in • p. 122

Ruby-throated Hummingbird
size 4 in • p. 124

Belted Kingfisher
size 12 in • p. 126

SHOREBIRDS

GULLS & TERNS

DOVES & CUCKOOS

OWLS

SWIFTS, HUMMINGBIRDS & KINGFISHERS

WOODPECKERS

Red-bellied Woodpecker
size 10 in • p. 128

Downy Woodpecker
size 6 in • p. 130

Northern Flicker
size 12 in • p. 132

FLYCATCHERS

Eastern Wood-Pewee
size 6 in • p. 134

Eastern Phoebe
size 7 in • p. 136

Great Crested Flycatcher
size 8 in • p. 138

VIREOS

Eastern Kingbird
size 9 in • p. 140

Red-eyed Vireo
size 6 in • p. 142

Blue Jay
size 11 in • p. 144

JAYS & CROWS

American Crow
size 19 in • p. 146

Fish Crow
size 15 in • p. 148

Purple Martin
size 7 in • p. 150

SWALLOWS

Tree Swallow
size 6 in • p. 152

Barn Swallow
size 7 in • p. 154

Carolina Chickadee
size 5 in • p. 156

CHICKADEES, NUTHATCHES & WRENS

Black-capped Chickadee
size 6 in • p. 158

Tufted Titmouse
size 6 in • p. 160

White-breasted Nuthatch
size 6 in • p. 162

CHICKADEES, NUTHATCHES & WRENS

Carolina Wren
size 5 in • p. 164

House Wren
size 5 in • p. 166

Eastern Bluebird
size 7 in • p. 168

BLUEBIRDS & THRUSHES

Hermit Thrush
size 7 in • p. 170

Wood Thrush
size 8 in • p. 172

American Robin
size 10 in • p. 174

MIMICS, STARLINGS & WAXWINGS

Gray Catbird
size 9 in • p. 176

Northern Mockingbird
size 10 in • p. 178

Brown Thrasher
size 11 in • p. 180

European Starling
size 8 in • p. 182

Cedar Waxwing
size 7 in • p. 184

Yellow Warbler
size 5 in • p. 186

WOOD-WARBLERS & TANAGERS

Yellow-rumped Warbler
size 5 in • p. 188

Black-and-white Warbler
size 5 in • p. 190

American Redstart
size 5 in • p. 192

Common Yellowthroat
size 5 in • p. 194

Scarlet Tanager
size 7 in • p. 196

Eastern Towhee
size 8 in • p. 198

Chipping Sparrow
size 6 in • p. 200

Song Sparrow
size 7 in • p. 202

SPARROWS, CARDINALS & BUNTINGS

White-throated Sparrow
size 7 in • p. 204

Dark-eyed Junco
size 6 in • p. 206

Northern Cardinal
size 8 in • p. 208

Rose-breasted Grosbeak
size 8 in • p. 210

Indigo Bunting
size 5 in • p. 212

Red-winged Blackbird
size 8 in • p. 214

BLACKBIRDS & ALLIES

Eastern Meadowlark
size 9 in • p. 216

Common Grackle
size 12 in • p. 218

Brown-headed Cowbird
size 7 in • p. 220

FINCHLIKE BIRDS

Baltimore Oriole
size 8 in • p. 222

House Finch
size 5 in • p. 224

American Goldfinch
size 5 in • p. 226

House Sparrow
size 6 in • p. 228

Introduction

If you have ever admired a songbird's pleasant notes, been fascinated by a soaring hawk or wondered how woodpeckers keep sawdust out of their nostrils, this book is for you. There is so much to discover about birds and their surroundings that birding is becoming one of the fastest growing hobbies on the planet. Many people find it relaxing, while others treat it as a sport. Some people enjoy its outdoor appeal and see it as a way to reconnect with nature, an opportunity to socialize with like-minded people or a way to monitor the environment.

Whether you are just beginning to take an interest in birds or can already identify many species, there is always more to learn. We've highlighted both the remarkable traits and the more typical behaviors displayed by some of our most abundant or noteworthy birds. A few of these birds live in specialized habitats, but most are common species that you have a good chance of encountering on most outings, or even in your own backyard.

BIRDING IN NEW JERSEY

We are truly blessed by the geographical and biological diversity of New Jersey. In addition to supporting a wide range of breeding birds

Northern Cardinal

and year-round residents, our state hosts a large number of spring and fall migrants that move through our area on the way to their breeding and wintering grounds. In all, 322 bird species have been seen and recorded in New Jersey.

Identifying birds in action and under varying conditions involves skill, timing and luck. The more you know about a bird—its range, preferred habitat, food preferences and hours and seasons of activity—the better your chances will be of seeing it. Generally, spring and fall are the busiest birding seasons. Temperatures are moderate then, many species of birds are on the move, and, in spring, male songbirds are belting out their unique courtship songs. Land birds are usually most active in the early morning hours, particularly during the warmest months of summer.

Another useful clue for correctly recognizing birds is knowledge of their preferred habitats. Simply put, a bird's habitat is the place where it normally lives. Some birds prefer open water, some are found in cattail marshes, others like mature coniferous forest and still other birds prefer abandoned agricultural fields overgrown with tall grass and shrubs. Habitats are just like neighborhoods: if you associate friends with the suburb in which they live, you can easily learn to associate specific birds with their preferred habitat. Only in migration, especially during inclement weather, do some birds leave their usual habitat.

Recognizing birds by their songs and calls can greatly enhance your birding experience. Numerous tapes and CDs are available to help you learn bird songs, and a portable player can let you quickly compare a live bird with a recording. The old-fashioned way to remember bird songs is to make up words for them. We have given you some of the classic renderings in the species accounts that follow. Some of these approximations work better than others; birds often add or delete syllables from their calls, and very few

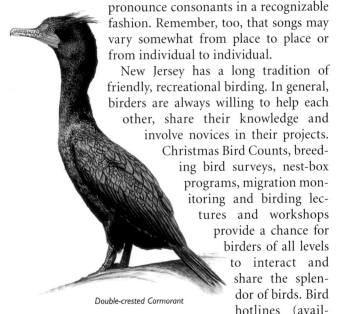

pronounce consonants in a recognizable fashion. Remember, too, that songs may vary somewhat from place to place or from individual to individual.

New Jersey has a long tradition of friendly, recreational birding. In general, birders are always willing to help each other, share their knowledge and involve novices in their projects. Christmas Bird Counts, breeding bird surveys, nest-box programs, migration monitoring and birding lectures and workshops provide a chance for birders of all levels to interact and share the splendor of birds. Bird hotlines (available on the web) provide up-to-date information on the sightings of rarities, which are often easier to relocate than you might think. For more information or to participate in these projects, contact the following organizations:

Double-crested Cormorant

New Jersey Audubon Society
9 Hardscrabble Road
Bernardsville, NJ 07924
www.njaudubon.org

Cape May Bird Observatory
600 Route 47 North
Cape May Court House, NJ 08210
(609) 861 0700

BIRD LISTING

Many birders list the species they have seen during their lifetime, for each year, each excursion taken, and/or for their own yard. It is up to you to decide what kind of list—systematic or casual—you will keep, and you may choose not to make lists at all. Lists may prove rewarding in unexpected ways, and after you visit a new area, your list becomes a souvenir of your experiences there. Keeping regular, accurate lists of birds at places you visit, including your own neighborhood, can also be useful for local researchers. It can be interesting to compare the arrival and departure dates of seasonal visitors from year to year, or to note the first-ever sighting of a new visitor to your area.

BIRD FEEDING

Many people set up bird feeders in their backyard, especially in winter. It is possible to attract specific birds by choosing the right kind of food and style of feeders. Keep your feeders stocked into early spring, because birds have a hard time finding food before the flowers bloom, seeds develop and insects hatch. Contrary to popular opinion, birds do not become dependent on feeders, nor do they subsequently forget to forage naturally. Be sure to clean your feeder and the surrounding area regularly to prevent the spread of disease.

Landscaping your property with native plants is another way of providing natural food for birds. Flocks of waxwings have a keen eye for red mountain-ash berries and hummingbirds enjoy sage and columbine flowers. The cumulative effects of "nature-scaping" urban and suburban yards can be a major step toward habitat conservation (especially when you consider that habitat is often lost in small amounts—a utility line is cut in one area and a highway is built in another). Many good books and websites about attracting wildlife to your backyard are available.

NEST BOXES

Another popular way to attract birds is to put up nest boxes, especially for House Wrens, Carolina Wrens, Eastern Bluebirds, Tree Swallows and Purple Martins. Not all birds will use nest boxes: only species that normally use cavities in trees are comfortable in such confined spaces. Larger nest boxes might attract kestrels, owls and cavity-nesting ducks.

WEST NILE VIRUS

Since the West Nile Virus first surfaced in North America in 1999, it has caused fear and misunderstanding. Some people have become afraid of contracting the disease from birds, and some health departments have advised residents to eliminate feeding stations and birdbaths.

To date, the disease has reportedly killed 284 species of birds. Corvids (crows, jays and ravens) and raptors have been the most obvious victims because of their size, though the disease also affects some smaller species. The virus is transmitted among birds and to humans (as well as some other mammals) by mosquitoes that have bitten infected birds. Birds do not get the disease directly from other birds, and humans cannot get it from casual contact with infected birds. As well, not all mosquito species can carry the disease. According to the Centers for Disease Control and Prevention

Red-bellied Woodpecker

(CDC), only about 20 percent of people who are bitten and become infected will develop any symptoms at all and less than 1 percent will become severely ill.

Because mosquitoes breed in standing water, birdbaths have the potential to become mosquito breeding grounds. Birdbaths should be emptied and have the water changed at least weekly. Drippers, circulating pumps, fountains or waterfalls that keep water moving will prevent mosquitoes from laying their eggs in the water. There are also bird-friendly products available to treat water in birdbaths. Contact your local nature store or garden center for more information on these products.

ABOUT THE SPECIES ACCOUNTS

This book gives detailed accounts of 105 species of birds that can be expected in New Jersey on an annual basis. The order of the birds and their common and scientific names follow the American Ornithologists' Union's *Check-list of North American Birds* (7th edition, July 1998, and its supplements through 2006).

As well as showing the identifying features of the bird, each species account also attempts to bring the bird to life by describing its various character traits. One of the challenges of birding is that many species look different in spring and summer than they do in fall and winter. Many birds have breeding and nonbreeding plumages, and immature birds often look different from the adults. This book does not try to describe or illustrate all the different plumages of a species; instead, it tries to focus on the forms that are most likely to be seen in our area.

ID: Large illustrations point out prominent field marks that will help you tell each species apart. The descriptions favor easily understood language instead of technical terms.

Other ID: This section lists additional identifying features. Some of the most common anatomical features of birds are pointed out in the Glossary illustration (p. 231).

Size: The average length of the bird's body from bill to tail, as well as its wingspan, are given and are approximate measurements of the bird as it is seen in nature. The size is sometimes given as a range, because there is variation between individuals, or between males and females.

Voice: You will hear many birds, particularly songbirds, which may remain hidden from view. Memorable paraphrases of distinctive sounds will aid you in identifying a species by ear.

Status: A general comment, such as "common," "uncommon" or "rare," is usually sufficient to describe the relative abundance of a species. Situations are bound to vary somewhat because migratory pulses, seasonal changes, changing weather conditions and centers of activity tend to concentrate or disperse birds.

Habitat: The habitats listed describe where each species is most commonly found. Because of the freedom that flight gives them, birds can turn up in almost any type of habitat. However, they will usually be found in environments that provide the specific food, water, cover and, in some cases, nesting habitat that they need to survive.

Similar Birds: Easily confused species are illustrated for each account. If you concentrate on the most relevant field marks, the subtle differences between species can be reduced to easily identifiable traits. Even experienced birders can mistake one species for another.

Nesting: In each species account, nest location and structure, clutch size, incubation period and parental duties are discussed. A photo of the bird's egg is also provided. Remember that birding ethics discourage the disturbance of active bird nests. If you disturb a nest, you may drive off the parents during a critical period or expose defenseless young to predators.

Range Maps: The range map for each species shows the overall range of the species in an average year. Most birds will confine their annual movements to this range, although each year some birds wander beyond their traditional boundaries. The maps show summer and winter ranges, as well as migratory pathways—areas of the state where birds may appear while en route to their nesting or wintering grounds. The representations of the pathways do not distinguish high-use migration corridors from areas that are used only occasionally.

Range Map Symbols

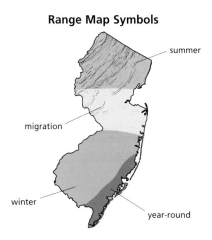

TOP BIRDING SITES

From the offshore waters and lowlands of the coastal plain to the mountainous northwest, our state can be separated into six natural regions: Offshore Waters, Outer Coastal Plain, Pine Barrens, Inner Coastal Plain, Piedmont and Highlands. Each region is composed of a number of different habitats that support a wealth of wildlife.

There are hundreds of good birding areas throughout our region. The following areas have been selected to represent a broad range of bird communities and habitats, with an emphasis on accessibility.

1. Cape May and Cape May County
2. Forsythe (Brigantine) NWR
3. Mannington Marsh/ Compromise Road
4. Lebanon and Wharton State Forests, Whitesbog
5. Palmyra Cove Nature Park
6. Brightview Farm
7. Tuckerton
8. Barnegat Light SP
9. Island Beach SP
10. Assunpink WMA
11. Shark River Estuary/ Manasquan Inlet
12. Thompson Park
13. Sandy Hook
14. DeKorte Park (Hackensack Meadowlands)
15. Great Swamp NWR
16. Scherman Hoffman Sanctuaries
17. Garret Mountain Reservation
18. Bull's Island
19. Alpha (borough)
20. Merrill Creek Reservoir
21. Pequannock Watershed
22. Wallkill River NWR
23. High Point SP

SP = State Park
WMA = Wildlife Management Area
NWR = National Wildlife Refuge

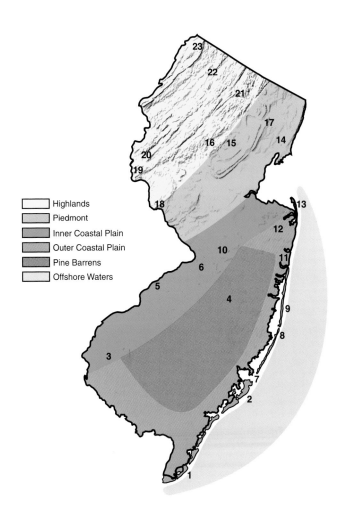

Highlands
Piedmont
Inner Coastal Plain
Outer Coastal Plain
Pine Barrens
Offshore Waters

Snow Goose
Chen caerulescens

Noisy flocks of Snow Geese can be quite entertaining, creating a moving patchwork in the sky with their black wing tips and white plumage. • These geese breed in the Arctic, some traveling as far as northeastern Siberia and crossing the Bering Strait twice a year. • Snow Geese can fly at speeds up to 20 miles per hour. They are also strong walkers, and mothers have been known to lead their goslings up to 45 miles on foot in search of suitable habitat. • The Snow Goose has two color morphs, a white and a blue, which until 1983 were considered two different species.

Other ID: head often stained rusty red. *Blue morph:* rare; white head and upper neck; dark blue-gray body. *In flight:* black wing tips.
Size: L 30–33 in; W 4½–5 ft.
Voice: loud, nasal, *houk-houk* in flight, higher pitched and more constant than that of the Canada Goose.
Status: uncommon to locally common migrant and winter visitor.
Habitat: croplands, fields, estuarine marshes.

Similar Birds

Ross's Goose

Look For

Snow Geese fly in wavy, disorganized lines, whereas Canada Geese fly in a V-formation. Occasionally mixed flocks form in migration.

black wing tips

dark "grin"
on bill

Nesting: does not nest in New Jersey; nests in the Arctic; female builds the nest and lines it with grass, feathers and down; creamy white eggs are 3⅛ x 2 in; female incubates 4–7 eggs for 22–25 days.

Did You Know?

While on their wintering grounds, Snow Geese spend up to 50 percent of the day feeding. Their smiling, serrated bills are made for grazing and gripping the slippery roots of marsh plants.

Canada Goose
Branta canadensis

Canada Geese mate for life and are devoted parents. Unlike most birds, the family stays together for nearly a year, which increases the survival rate of the young. Rescuers who care for injured geese report that these birds readily adopt their human caregivers. However, wild geese can be aggressive, especially when defending young or competing for food. Hissing sounds and low, outstretched necks are signs that you should give these birds some space. • The Canada Goose was split into two species in 2004. The larger subspecies are still known as Canada Geese. The smaller subspecies have been renamed Cackling Geese and are rare winter visitors to New Jersey.

Other ID: dark brown upperparts; light brown underparts. *In flight:* flocks fly in V-formation.
Size: L 3–4 ft; W up to 6 ft.
Voice: loud, familiar *ah-honk*.
Status: common permanent resident.
Habitat: lakeshores, riverbanks, ponds, farmlands and city parks.

Similar Birds

Cackling Goose

Brant

Greater White-fronted Goose

long, black neck

short, black tail

white "chin strap"

white undertail coverts

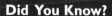

Nesting: usually on the ground; female builds a nest of grasses and mud and lines it with down; white eggs are 3½ x 2¼ in; female incubates 3–8 eggs for 25–28 days; goslings are born in early spring.

Did You Know?

Canada Geese graze on aquatic grasses and sprouts, but more often you see them grazing in farm fields and on large lawns.

Look For

Large flocks of Canada Geese migrate through New Jersey in October and November. The first downy goslings of the year are normally seen in late April.

Mute Swan
Cygnus olor

Admired for their grace and beauty, these Eurasian natives were introduced to eastern North America in the mid-1800s to adorn estates, zoos and city parks. Several escaped from captivity in New Jersey in 1916 and in New York shortly after, then soon began breeding in the wild. Over the years, Mute Swans have adapted well to the North American environment and have expanded their feral populations. Like many non-native species, Mute Swans are often fierce competitors for nesting areas and food sources. They can be very aggressive toward geese and ducks, often displacing many native species.

Other ID: *Immature:* white to grayish brown plumage; duller bill.
Size: *L* 5 ft; *W* 6¼ ft.
Voice: generally silent; may hiss or issue hoarse barking notes; loud wingbeats can be heard from up to ½ mile away.
Status: fairly common permanent resident.
Habitat: freshwater and brackish marshes, lakes and ponds.

Similar Birds

Tundra Swan

Snow Goose

neck is usually held
in an S-shape

bulbous, black
knob extends from
the forehead

wings are often
held in an arch
over the back
while swimming

all-white
plumage

orange bill
with a down-
turned tip

Nesting: on the ground along a shoreline;
female builds a mound of vegetation (male may
help gather material); pale green eggs are
4½ x 3 in; female incubates 5–10 eggs for about
36 days.

Did You Know?

Weighing in at 35 pounds,
as much as an average
4-year-old child, this large
swan is one of the conti-
nent's heaviest flying birds.

Look For

The adult Mute Swan's
orange bill with a black basal
knob, S-shaped neck and
slightly longer tail distinguish
it from our native Tundra
Swan.

Wood Duck
Aix sponsa

A forest-nesting species, the Wood Duck is equipped with fairly sharp claws for perching on branches and nesting in tree cavities. Shortly after hatching, the ducklings jump out of their nest cavity, often falling 20 feet or more. Like downy balls, they bounce on landing and are seldom injured. • Female Wood Ducks often return to the same nest site year after year, especially after successfully raising a brood. Established nest sites, where the adults are familiar with potential threats, may improve the young's chance of survival.

Other ID: long tail. *Male:* glossy green head with some white streaks; white-spotted, purplish chestnut breast; dark back and hindquarters. *Female:* gray-brown upperparts; white belly.
Size: L 15–20 in; W 30 in.
Voice: *Male:* ascending *ter-wee-wee. Female:* squeaky *woo-e-e-k.*
Status: fairly common local breeder and migrant; uncommon in winter.
Habitat: swamps, ponds, marshes and lakeshores with wooded edges.

Similar Birds

Hooded Merganser

Look For

Wood Ducks perch in trees and low overhanging riparian tangles more often than any other duck.

head raised
in flight

white, teardrop-
shaped eye patch

crest is slicked
back from crown

mottled brown
breast is streaked
with white

golden sides

black and white
shoulder slash

white chin
and throat

Nesting: in a hollow or tree cavity; may be as high as 30 ft up; also in an artificial nest box; usually near water; cavity is lined with down; white to buff eggs are 2⅛ x 1⅝ in; female incubates 9–14 eggs for 25–35 days.

Did You Know?

Hunting restrictions and thousands of nest boxes erected across its breeding range have helped the Wood Duck recover from dangerously low numbers.

Gadwall
Anas strepera

Gadwall numbers have recently reached record levels, with the North American population climbing to over 1.4 million breeding pairs in the early 21st century. • These medium-sized dabbling ducks are known for their lack of colorful plumage. Both sexes are grayish brown overall, with bold white wing patches. Males may be identified by their black rump and undertail coverts and females by their orange and brown bill and steep forehead.
• These ducks feed on a variety of aquatic plants and invertebrates and are typically found in deeper water, farther from shore than other dabbling ducks.

Other ID: *Male:* dark above with a grayish brown head; dark eyes and bill; yellow legs; black breast patch; gray flanks.
Size: *L* 18–22 in; *W* 33 in.
Voice: both sexes quack like a Mallard.
Status: uncommon to fairly common migrant and winter visitor; uncommon and local breeder.
Habitat: freshwater lakes or ponds; also brackish or saline ponds or estuaries in winter.

Similar Birds

American Wigeon

Mallard
(p. 32)

American Black Duck
(p. 30)

black tail and
upper- and
undertail coverts

white
speculum ♂

♀

brown bill
with orange
sides

♂

♀

gray or brown
overall

white belly

Nesting: well-concealed nest is a grassy,
down-lined hollow placed in tall vegetation,
sometimes far from water; creamy or pale
green eggs are 2¼ x 1½ in; female incubates
8–11 eggs for 24–27 days.

Did You Know?

Gadwalls form monoga-
mous pairs, and most
females have found a mate
by November, long before
the nesting season begins.

Look For

During winter, these ducks
feed in both freshwater and
brackish wetlands, often in
association with American
Wigeons and American
Coots.

American Black Duck
Anas rubripes

At home in lakes, beaver ponds and bogs, American Black Ducks breed in eastern Canada and the northeastern United States and winter from southeastern Canada to Florida. Like other puddle ducks, they forage by tipping up to reach food along the bottom of marshes and feed on a variety of seeds, aquatic plants, invertebrates and occasionally amphibians or small fish. • Populations of American Black Ducks are declining, partially as a result of hybridization with Mallards. Widespread Mallards are expanding their range and now overlap the American Black Duck over much of its breeding range. Habitat degradation is also contributing to the American Black Duck's decline.

Other ID: head and neck are paler than body; streaked throat. *Female:* olive bill. *In flight:* whitish underwings contrast with very dark body; violet speculum lacks white borders.
Size: *L* 20–24 in; *W* 35 in.
Voice: *Male:* a croak. *Female:* a loud quack.
Status: fairly common permanent resident; numbers augmented in winter.
Habitat: marshes, lakes, flooded agricultural fields.

Similar Birds

Mallard
(p. 32)

Gadwall
(p. 28)

dull yellowish bill

dark blackish body

orange-red legs and feet

Nesting: on the ground or rarely in a tree; nest of grasses and leaves is lined with down; pale cream, buff or greenish eggs are 2¼ x 1⅝ in; female incubates 8–10 eggs for 26–28 days.

Did You Know?

The scientific name *Anas* means "a duck," while *rubripes* means "red foot," referring to this duck's orange-red legs and feet.

Look For

Male and female American Black Ducks are very similar in appearance, which is unusual for waterfowl.

Mallard
Anas platyrhynchos

The male Mallard, with
his shiny green head and
chestnut brown breast, is the
classic puddle duck. • After
breeding, all male ducks lose their
elaborate plumage, helping them stay camouflaged
during their flightless period. By mid-fall, they
molt back into breeding colors. • Mallards will
freely hybridize with American Black Ducks as
well as domestic ducks. The resulting offspring are
a confusing blend of both parental types. • Resident
populations of feral Mallards are common in parks.

Other ID: orange legs and feet. *Male:* white
"necklace"; black tail feathers curl upward.
Female: mottled brown overall. *In flight:* dark
blue speculum bordered by white.
Size: *L* 20–28 in; *W* 3 ft.
Voice: quacks; female is louder than male.
Status: common permanent resident.
Habitat: lakes, wetlands, rivers, parks,
agricultural areas and sewage lagoons.

Similar Birds

Northern Shoveler

American Black Duck
(p. 30)

glossy, green head

yellow bill

♂

orange bill is spattered with black

♀

Nesting: grass nest is built on the ground or under a bush; creamy, grayish or greenish white eggs are 2¼ x 1⅝ in; female incubates 7–10 eggs for 26–30 days.

Did You Know?

A nesting hen generates enough body heat to make the grasses around her nest grow faster. She uses the tall grasses to further conceal her nest.

Look For

Mallards can be seen year-round, often in flocks and usually near open water. These confident ducks have even been caught dabbling in outdoor swimming pools.

Green-winged Teal
Anas crecca

Green-winged Teals, the smallest of our dabbling ducks, weigh less than a pound. They breed in estuaries and freshwater marshes throughout much of Alaska and Canada. Secluded breeding grounds likely contribute to their abundance, because they are among the most widely hunted ducks. • After breeding, male Green-winged Teals often undergo a partial migration before molting into their duller "eclipse" plumage.

Other ID: petite; small "scoop" bill. *Male:* pale gray sides; yellow undertail coverts. *Female:* mottled brown overall, with pale belly; variable dark eye line; pale undertail coverts.
Size: *L* 14 in; *W* 23 in.
Voice: male is quite vocal, uttering crisp, piping whistles; female quacks softly.
Status: fairly common migrant and winter visitor; rare and local breeder in the east
Habitat: a great variety of freshwater and estuarine habitats, favors shallow marshes with low cover.

Similar Birds

Blue-winged Teal

Look For

In flight, the teal's small size, dark body and habit of "turning the corner" tightly in wheeling flocks resembles the flight of shorebirds.

green speculum

chestnut head with a glossy green swipe that extends back from the eye

dusky stripes on face

♂

♀

vertical white shoulder slash

creamy breast spotted with black

Nesting: does not nest in New Jersey; nests in Alaska and northern Canada; on the ground, well concealed in tall vegetation; nest built of grass and leaves is lined with down; creamy white eggs are 1⅗ x 1¼ in; female incubates 6–11 eggs over about 21 days.

Did You Know?

The name "teal" possibly originated from the medieval English word *tele* or the old Dutch word *teling*, each of which means "small." There are 16 species of teals worldwide.

Greater Scaup
Aythya marila

Two scaup species occur in New Jersey, but the Greater Scaup is usually more common and widespread, particularly along the coast. The primary field mark to separate the scaup can be seen when the birds are in flight or when stretching their wings. The white wing stripe of the secondary flight feathers extends onto the primaries on the Greater Scaup but is a dull gray on the primaries of the Lesser Scaup.

Other ID: golden eyes. *Male:* light gray back; dark hindquarters. *Female:* brown overall; well-defined white patch at base of bill.
Size: L 18 in; W 28 in.
Voice: generally silent; male gives a soft whistle, and female purrs during courtship.
Status: fairly common to locally common migrant and winter visitor with the largest numbers along the coast.
Habitat: large lakes and reservoirs, marshes and nearshore ocean.

Similar Birds

Lesser Scaup

Ring-necked Duck

white wing stripe extends well into primary feathers

iridescent dark green head (often appears black)

rounded or flat-topped head

blue, black-tipped bill

white belly and flanks

dark breast

Nesting: does not nest in New Jersey; nests in Alaska and northern Canada; on the ground, in a depression lined with vegetation and feathers; pale olive eggs are 2½ x 1¾ in; female incubates 6–15 eggs for 24–28 days.

Did You Know?

The Greater Scaup can remain underwater for one minute and dive to depths of 20 feet.

Look For

Scaup are diving ducks that use their large feet and rear-placed legs to propel themselves underwater.

Surf Scoter
Melanitta perspicillata

Scoters are darkly plumaged sea ducks that feed on shellfish and barnacles. Males have brightly colored, bulbous bills. Three species occur in North America, and all are usually found off the New Jersey coast during migration and winter. The largest numbers occur from October to November and again in March. • Surf Scoters are the only scoters that breed and winter exclusively in North America. To take advantage of the short summer, they pair up before arriving on their summer breeding grounds.

Other ID: *Male:* black overall; orange legs. *Female:* 2 whitish patches on sides of head; brown overall.
Size: *L* 17–21 in; *W* 28–31 in.
Voice: generally quiet; occasionally utters low, harsh croaks. *Male:* occasionally gives a low, clear whistle. *Female:* guttural *krraak krraak.*
Status: common migrant and winter visitor along the coast; very rare inland.
Habitat: bays, inlets and nearshore ocean waters; large, deep lakes in the interior.

Similar Birds

White-winged Scoter

Black Scoter
(p. 40)

sloping forehead

dark gray bill

♀

white on forehead
and back of neck

♂

black spot, outlined in
white at base of bill

Nesting: does not nest in New Jersey; nests in
the Arctic; in a shallow scrape under bushes,
near water; nest is lined with down; buff-
colored eggs are 2½ x 1⅝ in; female incubates
5–9 eggs for 28–30 days.

Did You Know?

The Surf Scoter is often
called "Skunkhead"
because of the male's
striking white head
patches.

Look For

Huge rafts of Surf Scoters
and Black Scoters assemble
off beaches and headlands
and around harbor entrances.

Black Scoter
Melanitta nigra

The Black Scoter sits like a sturdy buoy on the waves of nearshore ocean waters, bays, inlets and large lakes. This bird breeds in Alaska and northern Canada and is well adapted to life on rough waters, spending winters just beyond the breaking surf on the Atlantic and Pacific coasts. • The male Black Scoter is the only adult duck in North America with entirely black plumage. Though American Coots also have black plumage, they belong to the rail family and are found in freshwater and brackish wetlands.

Other ID: *Female:* dark brown overall; large, pale patch on face, cheeks and upper neck; dark bill. *In flight:* silvery flash in wing.
Size: *L* 17–20 in; *W* 28 in.
Voice: mostly silent in New Jersey; wings whistle in flight.
Status: common migrant and winter visitor along the coast; rare inland.
Habitat: ocean, estuaries and bays; occasionally at larger lakes and reservoirs.

Similar Birds

White-winged Scoter

Surf Scoter
(p. 38)

Ruddy Duck

black overall

large yellow-orange knob on bill

♂

♀

♂

♀

Nesting: does not breed in New Jersey; nests in the Arctic and Atlantic Canada; on the ground near water, in a depression lined with grass and down; light to pinkish buff eggs are 2½ x 1¾ in; female incubates 6–10 eggs for 27–31 days.

Did You Know?

Scoters wrench shellfish off underwater rocks or the sea floor. They swallow mollusks whole and grind the shells in their muscular gizzards.

Look For

While resting on the water's surface, Black Scoters tend to hold their bills parallel to the water, whereas other scoters tend to hold their bills downward.

Long-tailed Duck

Clangula hyemalis

When spring breakup begins in the Arctic, groups of Long-tailed Ducks gather on open water, interrupting the stillness with constant, melodious chatter. • The breeding and nonbreeding plumages of these ducks are like photo-negatives of each other: the spring breeding plumage is mostly dark with white highlights; the winter plumage is mostly white with dark patches. The handsome males retain their long tail feathers throughout the year.

Other ID: *Breeding male:* dark head with a white eye patch; dark neck and upperparts; white belly. *Breeding female:* short tail feathers; gray bill; dark crown, throat patch, wings and back; white underparts.
Size: *L* 16½–21 in; *W* 28 in.
Voice: courtship call—*owl-owl-owlet*—is rarely heard outside the breeding range.
Status: fairly common migrant and winter visitor along the coast; rare inland.
Habitat: bays, estuaries and ocean; rarely inland on large, deep lakes.

Similar Birds

Northern Pintail   Bufflehead

nonbreeding

generally lighter, especially on head

pale head with dark cheek patch

long, dark central tail feathers

long, white patches on back

♂

♀

dark bill

pink bill with dark base

nonbreeding

pale neck and belly

Nesting: does not nest in New Jersey; nests in the Arctic; on dry ground near water; depression in the ground is lined with plant material and down; olive gray to olive buff eggs are 2 x 1½ in; female incubates 5–11 eggs for 24–29 days.

Did You Know?

Long-tailed Ducks and King Eiders are among the world's deepest-diving waterfowl—both make regular dives to depths of more than 200 feet.

Look For

These ducks tend to remain slightly offshore, limiting observers to brief glimpses of their winter finery and the male's long, slender tail feathers.

Common Merganser
Mergus merganser

Lumbering like a jumbo jet, the Common Merganser must run along the surface of the water, beating its heavy wings to gain sufficient lift to take off. Once up and away, this large duck flies arrow-straight and low over the water, making broad, sweeping turns to follow the meandering shorelines of rivers and lakes. • Common Mergansers are highly social and often gather in large groups during migration. In winter, any source of open water with a fish-filled shoal will support good numbers of these skilled divers.

Other ID: large, elongated body. *Male:* white body plumage; black stripe on back; dark eyes.
Female: gray body; orangy eyes. *In flight:* shallow wingbeats; body is compressed and arrowlike.
Size: L 22–27 in; W 34 in.
Voice: *Male:* harsh *uig-a,* like a guitar twang.
Female: harsh *karr karr.*
Status: common migrant and winter visitor in the north; scarce in the south; scarce breeder.
Habitat: large rivers and deep lakes.

Similar Birds

Red-breasted
Merganser

Hooded Merganser

Common Loon
(p. 48)

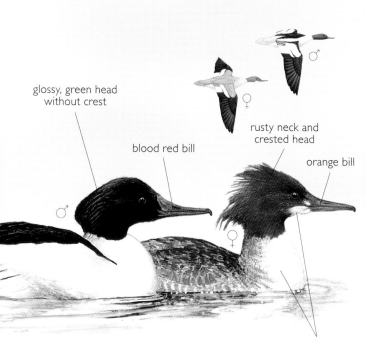

glossy, green head
without crest

rusty neck and
crested head

blood red bill

orange bill

♂

♀

♀

clean white chin
and breast

Nesting: in a tree cavity or occasionally on the ground, on a cliff ledge or in a large nest box; usually close to water; pale buff eggs are 2½ x 1¾ in; female incubates 8–11 eggs for 30–35 days.

Did You Know?

The Common Merganser is the most widespread merganser in North America. It also occurs in Europe and Asia.

Look For

You may see the Common Merganser with only its head underwater, searching for prey. This duck's serrated bill allows it to grip slippery fish.

Wild Turkey
Meleagris gallopavo

The Wild Turkey was once common throughout most of eastern North America, but in the early 20th century, habitat loss and overhunting took a toll on this bird. Today, efforts at restoration have re-established the Wild Turkey in many areas, including New Jersey. • This charismatic bird is the only native North American animal that has been widely domesticated. • Early in life both male and female turkeys gobble. The females outgrow this practice, leaving the males to gobble competitively for the honor of mating.

Other ID: dark, glossy, iridescent body plumage; largely unfeathered legs. *Male:* black-tipped breast feathers. *Female:* smaller; grayer head; less iridescent body; brown-tipped breast feathers.
Size: *Male: L* 3–3½ ft; *W* 5½ ft. *Female: L* 3 ft; *W* 4 ft.
Voice: courting male gobbles loudly; alarm call is a loud *pert;* gathering call is a cluck; contact call is a loud *keouk-keouk-keouk.*
Status: uncommon to fairly common permanent resident.
Habitat: deciduous, mixed and riparian woodlands; woodland edges; occasionally grain and corn fields during late fall and winter.

Similar Birds

Ring-necked Pheasant

Look For

Eastern Wild Turkeys have brown or rusty tail tips and are slimmer than domestic turkeys, which have white tail tips.

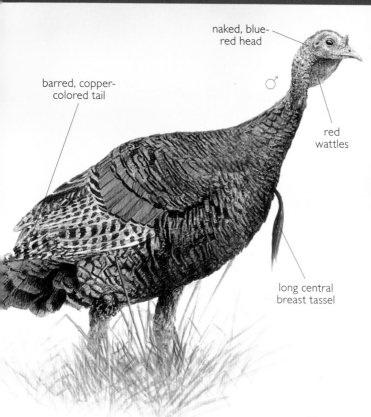

naked, blue-red head

barred, copper-colored tail

♂

red wattles

long central breast tassel

Nesting: in a woodland or at a field edge; nests on the ground, in a depression under thick cover; nest is lined with grass and leaves; brown-speckled, pale buff eggs are 2½ x 1¾ in; female incubates 10–12 eggs for up to 28 days.

Did You Know?

If Congress had taken Benjamin Franklin's advice in 1782, our national emblem would be the Wild Turkey instead of the Bald Eagle. As it was, the Bald Eagle beat out the Wild Turkey by only one congressional vote.

Common Loon
Gavia immer

Common Loons are well suited to their aquatic lifestyle. These divers have nearly solid bones that make them less buoyant (most birds have hollow bones), and their feet are placed well back on their bodies for underwater propulsion. Small bass, perch and sunfish are all fair game for these excellent underwater hunters. • A loon's heavy body and relatively small wing size mean it requires a lengthy sprint over water before taking off. • In winter, look for these divers near shore up and down the coast and on larger bays and reservoirs.

Other ID: *Breeding:* green-black head; white "necklace"; black and white "checkerboard" upperparts; white breast and underparts. *Nonbreeding:* dull dark gray plumage; light underparts; dark patch on side of neck. *In flight:* long wings beat constantly; legs and large feet trail behind tail; hunchbacked appearance.
Size: *L* 28–35 in; *W* 4–5 ft.
Voice: generally silent in winter; alarm call is a quavering tremolo.
Status: fairy common migrant and winter visitor.
Habitat: ocean, brackish sounds and lakes and ponds.

Similar Birds

Red-throated Loon

Double-breasted Cormorant (p. 54)

Red-breasted Merganser

pale
eye-arcs

dark eyes

heavy, dagger-
like bill

white
underparts

nonbreeding

Nesting: does not nest in New Jersey; nests in New England, the Great Lakes region and Canada; nest is a mound of aquatic vegetation; darkly spotted, olive brown eggs are 3½ x 2¼ in; pair incubates 1–3 eggs for 24–31 days.

Did You Know?

Loons will chase fish to depths of 180 feet—as deep as an Olympic-sized swimming pool is long.

Look For

Rear-placed legs make walking on land awkward for these birds. The word "loon" is probably derived from the Scandinavian word *lom,* which means "clumsy person."

Horned Grebe
Podiceps auritus

breeding

Grebes are like small varieties of loons, which they resemble in their plain plumage and diving habits. Horned Grebes are found locally in New Jersey during winter, occurring along the coast and on large inland lakes. They ride high in the water and have a flat head outline. • This bird's English name and its scientific name, *auritus* (eared), refer to the golden feather tufts that these grebes acquire in breeding plumage—a plumage that is seldom seen in New Jersey.

Other ID: *Breeding:* yellow "ear" tufts; black cheek and foreneck; rufous neck and sides; gray back. *In flight:* wings beat constantly; large white patch at rear of inner wing.
Size: *L* 12–15 in; *W* 18 in.
Voice: silent in New Jersey.
Status: uncommon to fairly common migrant and winter visitor.
Habitat: mainly coastal waters; also large inland lakes.

Similar Birds

Pied-billed Grebe   Red-necked Grebe

flat, black crown

white cheek
and foreneck

tip of bill is
usually pale

blackish gray
upperparts

nonbreeding

light underparts

Nesting: does not breed in New Jersey; nests
in western Canada, Alaska and spottily in the
north-central U.S.; usually singly or in small
groups; nest is a mound of rotting vegetation in
shallow water; white eggs are 1⅝ x 1¼ in; pair
incubates 3–5 eggs for 22–25 days.

Did You Know?

Grebes catch their food in
long dives that may last up
to three minutes, and they
can travel as far as 400
feet under water.

Look For

Unlike the fully webbed front
toes of most swimming birds,
the toes of grebes are individually webbed, or lobed.

Northern Gannet
Morus bassanus

The Northern Gannet, with its elegant face mask and high forehead, slices through the open ocean air with blackened wing tips. • These gentle-looking birds do not breed until they are at least five years of age, and they mate for life. To re-establish their bond each year, pairs affectionately dip their bills to the breast of their mate, bow, raise their wings and preen each other. • Squadrons of gannets soaring at heights of more than 100 feet above the water will suddenly fold their wings back and simultaneously plunge headfirst into the ocean depths in pursuit of schooling fish.

Other ID: white overall; long, narrow wings; pointed tail; black feet. *Immature:* mottled gray, black and white.
Size: *L* 3–3¼ ft; W 6 ft.
Voice: usually silent at sea; feeding flocks may exchange grating growls.
Status: fairly common to common migrant and winter visitor.
Habitat: roosts and feeds in open ocean waters most of the year; often seen well off-shore; regularly seen from shore during migration.

Similar Birds

Snow Goose
(p. 20)

Look For

Gannets may be seen in lines, small groups or as individuals, flying offshore with steady wingbeats and occasionally plunge diving.

juvenile

thick, tapered, pale gray bill

buffy wash on nape

black wing tips

Nesting: does not nest in New Jersey; nests on islands in the Atlantic provinces of Canada; in a shallow hollow on a mound of material, usually seaweed, lined with feathers and other plants; dull, chalky white egg is 3¼ x 2 in; pair incubates 1 egg (rarely 2) for 43–45 days.

Did You Know?

Gannets are pelagic birds that spend most of the year away from land, feeding and roosting at sea. Only during the breeding season do they seek out land to lay their eggs and raise their young in large sea-cliff colonies.

Double-crested Cormorant

Phalacrocorax auritus

The Double-crested Cormorant looks like a bird but smells and swims like a fish. With a long, rudderlike tail and excellent underwater vision, this slick-feathered bird has mastered the underwater world. Most water birds have waterproof feathers, but the structure of the Double-crested Cormorant's feathers allows water in. "Wettable" feathers make this bird less buoyant, which in turn makes it a better diver. The Double-crested Cormorant also has sealed nostrils for diving and therefore must fly with its bill slightly open.

Other ID: all-black body; blue eyes. *Immature:* brown upperparts; pale throat and breast; yellowish orange throat patch. *In flight:* rapid wingbeats; kinked neck.
Size: L 26–32 in; W 4¼ ft.
Voice: generally quiet; may issue piglike grunts or croaks, especially near nest colonies.
Status: fairly common to common migrant; uncommon winter visitor; uncommon in summer, usually as a nonbreeder
Habitat: large lakes and large, meandering rivers.

Similar Birds

Great Cormorant

Common Loon
(p. 48)

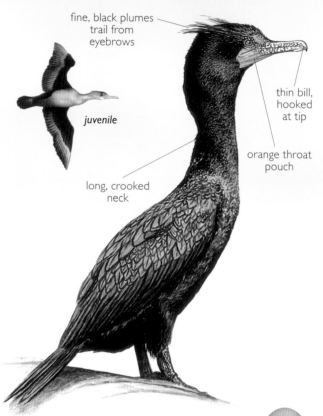

fine, black plumes trail from eyebrows

thin bill, hooked at tip

juvenile

orange throat pouch

long, crooked neck

Nesting: rare and very local breeder; nests in northern U.S. and Canada; colonial; on an island or high in a tree; platform nest is made of sticks and guano; pale blue eggs are 2 x 1½ in; both sexes incubate 2–7 eggs for 25–30 days.

Did You Know?

Japanese fishermen sometimes use cormorants on leashes to catch fish. This traditional method of fishing is called *ukai*.

Look For

Double-crested Cormorants often perch on pilings, buoys or piers with their wings partially spread. Lacking oil glands, they use the wind to dry their feathers.

Great Blue Heron
Ardea herodias

The Great Blue Heron is the tallest of all herons and egrets in North America. This long-legged bird has a stealthy, often motionless hunting strategy. It waits for a fish or frog to approach and spears the prey with its bill, then may flip its catch into the air and swallow it whole. This heron usually hunts near water, but it also stalks fields and meadows in search of rodents. • Great Blue Herons settle in communal treetop nests called rookeries. Nesting herons are sensitive to human disturbance, so observe this bird's behavior from a distance.

Other ID: blue-gray overall; long, dark legs; plumes streak from throat. *In flight:* slow, steady wingbeats; black upperwing tips; legs trail behind body.
Size: L 4¼–4½ ft; W 6 ft.
Voice: quiet away from the nest; occasional harsh *frahnk frahnk frahnk* during takeoff.
Status: fairly common migrant and winter visitor; uncommon breeder.
Habitat: forages along edges of rivers, lakes and marshes; also in fields and wet meadows.

Similar Birds

Little Blue Heron

Look For

In flight, the Great Blue Heron folds its neck back over its shoulders in an S-shape. Similar-looking cranes stretch their necks out when flying.

neck folds back over shoulders

black plumes above eye

yellow bill

long, curving neck with black markings on throat

chestnut brown thighs

Nesting: colonial; adds to stick platform nest over years; nest width can reach 4 ft; pale bluish green eggs are 2½ x 1¾ in; pair incubates 4–7 eggs for approximately 28 days.

Did You Know?

Because they frequent areas visited by people—rivers, lakeshores, beaches, sand flats, piers and even some urban parks—Great Blue Herons are seen more often at close range than any other heron.

Great Egret
Ardea alba

The plumes of Great Egrets and Snowy Egrets were widely used to decorate hats in the early 20th century. An ounce of egret feathers cost as much as $32—more than an ounce of gold at that time— and, as a result, egret populations began to disappear. Some of the first conservation legislation in North America was enacted to outlaw the hunting of Great Egrets. These birds are now recovering and expanding their range, probably back into areas where they formerly nested, though the loss of wetland habitat is an ongoing problem. • These beautiful birds can be found in coastal marshes and locally inland.

Other ID: all-white plumage. *Breeding:* white plumes trail from rump; green skin patch between eyes and base of bill. *In flight:* neck folds back over shoulders; legs extend backward.
Size: L 3–3½ ft; W 4 ft.
Voice: rapid, low-pitched, loud *cuk-cuk-cuk*.
Status: fairly common migrant and breeder along the coast, uncommon inland.
Habitat: marshes, open riverbanks, irrigation canals and lakeshores.

Similar Birds

Snowy Egret
(p. 60)

Cattle Egret

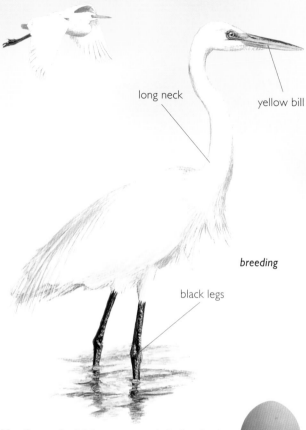

long neck

yellow bill

breeding

black legs

Nesting: colonial, but may nest in isolated pairs; in a tree or tall shrub; pair builds a platform of sticks; pale blue-green eggs are 2¼ x 1⅝ in; pair incubates 3–5 eggs for 23–26 days.

Did You Know?

The Great Egret is the symbol for the National Audubon Society, one of the oldest conservation organizations in the United States.

Look For

Like the Great Blue Heron, the Great Egret sometimes feeds on rodents in fields and pastures.

Snowy Egret

Egretta thula

Looking as if it stepped in a can of yellow paint, the dainty Snowy Egret flaunts famously yellow feet on black legs. Come breeding season, long plumes extend from its neck and back. This bird was perhaps the most sought-after target for the plume trade because of the abundance of its fine aigrettes. • Like other wading birds, Snowy Egrets teetered on the brink of extirpation in New Jersey by the early 1900s. Their populations have recovered dramatically, and they now occur locally beyond their historical range limits in North America, although declining numbers since the 1980s are a cause for concern.

Other ID: medium-sized, white wading bird.
Size: *L* 22–26 in; *W* 3½ ft.
Voice: generally silent away from colonies.
Status: fairly common migrant and breeder along the coast; rare inland.
Habitat: marshes, edges of rivers, lakes and ponds.

Similar Birds

Great Egret
(p. 58)

Cattle Egret

yellow lores

nonbreeding

black bill

long plumes
on throat and
lower back

black legs

bright yellow
feet

Nesting: colonial; in a tree or tall shrub; pair
builds a platform of sticks; pale blue-green eggs
are 1⅝ x 1¼ in; pair incubates 3–5 eggs for
23–26 days.

Did You Know?

These birds feed by
actively chasing prey or
by poking their bright
yellow feet in the muck
of shallow wetlands,
flushing out prey.

Look For

Foraging egrets sometimes
extend their wings over open
water to create shade, which
provides better visibility and
attracts fish seeking shelter
from the sun.

Green Heron
Butorides virescens

A sentinel of pond edges and small marshes, the ever-vigilant Green Heron sits hunched on a shaded branch at the water's edge. This crow-sized heron stalks frogs and small fish lurking in the weedy shallows, then stabs them with its bill. • Unlike most herons, the Green Heron nests singly rather than communally, though it can sometimes be found in loose colonies. While some of this heron's habitat has been lost to wetland drainage or channelization, the building of farm ponds or reservoirs has created habitat in other areas.

Other ID: stocky body; relatively short, yellow-green legs; bill is dark above and greenish below; short tail. *Breeding male:* bright orange legs. *Immature:* heavy streaking along neck and underparts; dark brown upperparts.
Size: *L* 15–22 in; *W* 26 in.
Voice: generally silent; alarm and flight calls are a loud *kowp, kyow* or *skow;* aggression call is a harsh *raah.*
Status: uncommon to fairly common migrant and breeder.
Habitat: marshes, lakes and streams with dense shoreline or emergent vegetation.

Similar Birds

Black-crowned
Night-Heron

Least Bittern

American Bittern

dark, iridescent back

green-black crown

chestnut face and neck

Nesting: nests singly or in small, loose groups; platform nest in a tree or shrub, usually by water; pale blue-green eggs are 1½ x 1⅛ in; pair incubates 3–5 eggs for 19–21 days.

Did You Know?

Herons of the *Butorides* genus have been seen baiting fish to the water's surface by dropping small bits of debris such as twigs or vegetation.

Look For

The Green Heron often appears bluish or black; the iridescent green shine on its back and outer wings is only visible in certain light.

Glossy Ibis

Plegadis falcinellus

The exotic look of the Glossy Ibis hints of its distant West Africa origins. The powerful trade winds that drew Christopher Columbus to North America most likely also guided this graceful bird to the warm, productive Caribbean only a few centuries ago. In the 1930s, the Glossy Ibis established a small breeding colony in Florida's rich coastal marshes, then quickly expanded its range up the East Coast, with breeding documented north to Maine. Recent population declines, however, are a cause of concern.

Other ID: *Breeding:* chestnut head, neck and sides; green and purple sheen on wings, tail, crown and face. *Nonbreeding:* dark grayish brown head and neck are streaked with white. *In flight:* hunchbacked appearance, legs trail behind tail.
Size: *L* 22–25 in; *W* 3 ft.
Voice: cooing accompanies billing and preening during nest relief.
Status: uncommon to fairly common migrant and summer breeder; rare inland.
Habitat: freshwater and saltwater marshes, swamps, flooded fields and shallow estuaries with adequate shoreline vegetation for nesting.

Similar Birds

Little Blue Heron

Look For

Flocks of Glossy Ibises fly in lines or V-formations, and individuals hold their neck fully extended in flight.

nonbreeding

long, down-curved bill

dark skin in front of brown eye is bordered by 2 pale stripes

breeding

long legs

Nesting: in colonies, often intermixed with egrets and herons; bulky platform of marsh vegetation and sticks is built over water, on the ground or on top of a tall shrub or small tree; new material is added to nest until young fledge; pale blue or green eggs are 2 x 1½ in; pair incubates 3–4 eggs for approximately 21 days.

Did You Know?

The Glossy Ibis is most often seen sweeping its head back and forth through the water, skillfully using its long, sickle-shaped bill to probe the marshland mud for unseen prey.

Turkey Vulture
Cathartes aura

Turkey Vultures are intelligent and social birds. Groups live and sleep together in large trees, or "roosts." Some roost sites are over a century old and have been used by the same family of vultures for several generations. • The genus name *Cathartes* means "cleanser" and refers to this bird's affinity for carrion. A vulture's bill and feet are much less powerful than those of an eagle, hawk or falcon, which kill live prey. Its red, featherless head may appear grotesque, but this adaptation allows the bird to stay relatively clean while feeding on messy carcasses.

Other ID: *Immature:* gray head. *In flight:* head appears small; silver gray flight feathers; rocks from side-to-side when soaring.
Size: L 25–31 in; W 5½–6 ft.
Voice: generally silent; occasionally produces a hiss or grunt if threatened.
Status: fairly common to common permanent resident; local in winter in the north.
Habitat: usually flies over open country, shorelines or roads; rarely over forests.

Similar Birds

Black Vulture   Golden Eagle   Bald Eagle, immature

wings are held in
a shallow "V."

bare, red head

brownish overall

pale, hooked bill

Nesting: in a cave, crevice, log or among
boulders; uses no nest material; dull white or
creamy, brown spotted eggs are 2¾ x 2 in; pair
incubates 2 eggs for up to 41 days.

Did You Know?

A threatened Turkey
Vulture will often throw
up. The odor of its vomit
repulses attackers, much
like the odor of a skunk's
spray does.

Look For

Turkey Vultures often hop
or run along the ground,
especially when competing
for a carcass.

Osprey

Pandion haliaetus

The large, powerful Osprey is almost always found near water. While hunting for fish, this bird hovers in the air before hurling itself toward the water in a dramatic headfirst dive. An instant before striking the water, it rights itself and thrusts its feet forward to grasp its quarry. The Osprey has specialized feet for gripping slippery prey—two toes point forward, two point backward and all are covered with sharp spines. • The Osprey is one of the most widely distributed birds in the world—it is found on every continent except Antarctica.

Other ID: dark "necklace" may be absent; yellow eyes; pale crown; gray feet. *Male:* all-white throat. *Female:* more prominent dark "necklace." *Immature:* finely speckled with pale spots above. *In flight:* long wings are held in a shallow "M"; dark "wrist" patches; brown and white tail bands.
Size: *L* 22–25 in; *W* 5½–6 ft.
Voice: series of melodious ascending whistles: *chewk-chewk-chewk;* also a familiar *kip-kip-kip.*
Status: fairly common migrant and breeder in coastal areas; uncommon and local inland.
Habitat: salt marshes and estuaries; lakes and slow-flowing rivers and streams.

Similar Birds

Bald Eagle   Rough-legged Hawk

dark eye line

gray bill

long wings
extend past tail

Nesting: on a treetop or artificial structure, usually near water; massive stick nest is reused annually; yellowish, brown-blotched eggs are $2\frac{3}{8} \times 1\frac{3}{4}$ in; pair incubates 2–4 eggs for 38 days.

Did You Know?

The Osprey's dark eye line blocks the glare of the sun on the water, allowing the bird to spot fish near the water's surface.

Look For

Ospreys build bulky nests on artificial structures such as communication towers, utility poles, buoys, channel markers and raised platforms specifically built for them.

Northern Harrier
Circus cyaneus

With its prominent white rump and distinctive slightly upturned wings, the Northern Harrier may be the easiest raptor to identify in flight. It often flies close to the ground, relying on sudden surprise attacks to capture prey. • The courtship flight of the Northern Harrier is a spectacle worth watching in spring. The male climbs almost vertically in the air, then stalls and plummets in a reckless dive toward the ground. At the last second, he saves himself with a hairpin turn that sends him skyward again.

Other ID: *Male:* pale gray to silver gray upperparts; white underparts; indistinct tail bands, except for 1 dark subterminal band. *Female:* dark brown upperparts; streaky, brown and buff underparts. *Immature:* warm brown overall. *In flight:* long wings and tail; black wing tips; white rump.
Size: *L* 16–24 in; *W* 3½–4 ft.
Voice: generally quiet; high-pitched *ke-ke-ke-ke-ke-ke* near the nest or during courtship.
Status: uncommon migrant and winter visitor; rare and local breeder.
Habitat: open country, including marshes, fields, wet meadows, bogs and croplands.

Similar Birds

Rough-legged Hawk

Red-tailed Hawk (p. 78)

Peregrine Falcon

Short-eared Owl

facial disc

♂

♀

yellow legs

long, dark-banded tail

Nesting: on the ground; usually in tall vegetation or on a raised mound; shallow depression is lined with grass, sticks and cattails; bluish white eggs are 1⅞ x 1⅜ in; female incubates 4–6 eggs for 30–32 days.

Did You Know?

Britain's Royal Air Force was so impressed by the Northern Harrier's maneuverability that it named the Harrier aircraft after this bird.

Look For

The Northern Harrier's owl-like, parabolic facial disc enhances its hearing, allowing this bird to hunt by sound as well as by sight.

Sharp-shinned Hawk

Accipiter striatus

After a successful hunt, the small Sharp-shinned Hawk often perches on a favorite "plucking post" with its meal in its razor-sharp talons. This hawk is a member of the *Accipter* genus, or woodland hawks, and it preys almost exclusively on small birds. Its short, rounded wings, long, rudderlike tail and flap-and-glide flight allow it to maneuver through woodlands at high speed.

Other ID: red eyes; blue-gray back and upperwings.
Immature: browner upperparts; darkly streaked underparts. *In flight:* small head; short neck; short, rounded wings; dark barring on flight feathers.
Size: *Male: L* 10–12 in; *W* 20–24 in. *Female: L* 12–14 in; *W* 24–28 in.
Voice: usually silent; intense, repeated *kik-kik-kik-kik* during the breeding season.
Status: uncommon to fairly common migrant and winter visitor; rare breeder.
Habitat: dense to semi-open forests and large woodlots; occasionally along rivers and in suburban areas; favors bogs and dense, moist, coniferous forests for nesting.

Similar Birds

Cooper's Hawk
(p. 74)

American Kestrel
(p. 80)

Merlin

blue-gray crown

red horizontal bars
on underparts

immature

long, heavily barred,
square-tipped tail

Nesting: in a conifer; builds a new stick nest
or uses an abandoned crow nest; brown-
blotched, bluish white eggs are 1½ x 1⅛ in;
female incubates 4–5 eggs for 34–35 days;
male feeds the female during incubation.

Did You Know?

As it ages, the Sharp-
shinned Hawk's bright yellow eyes become red.
This change may signal full
maturity to potential
mates.

Look For

After a successful hunt, the
Sharp-shinned Hawk usually
perches on a favorite "plucking post," grasping its meal in
its talons.

Cooper's Hawk
Accipiter cooperii

The Cooper's Hawk quickly changes the scene at a backyard bird feeder when it comes looking for a meal. European Starlings, American Robins and House Sparrows are among its favorite
immature choices of prey. • You might also spot this songbird scavenger hunting along forest edges. It is capable of maneuvering quickly at high speeds and uses surprise and speed to snatch its prey in midair.

Other ID: short, rounded wings; dark barring on pale underwings; blue-gray back; pale terminal tail band. *Immature:* brown upperparts; russet-brown on nape; darkly streaked underparts.
Size: *Male: L* 15–17 in; *W* 27–32 in.
Female: L 17–19 in; *W* 32–37 in.
Voice: fast, woodpecker-like *cac-cac-cac-cac.*
Status: uncommon permanent resident; fairly common in migration and winter.
Habitat: mixed woodlands, riparian woodlands and urban gardens with feeders.

Similar Birds

Sharp-shinned Hawk
(p. 72)

American Kestrel
(p. 80)

Merlin

squarish head

red eyes

red, horizontal barring
on underparts

long, straight,
heavily barred,
rounded tail

Nesting: nest of sticks is built
20–65 ft high in a deciduous or
coniferous tree, often near a
stream or pond; might add to
an abandoned crow nest; bluish
white eggs are 2 x 1½ in; female
incubates 3–5 eggs for 34–36
days; male feeds female during
incubation.

Did You Know?

Most female birds of prey
are larger than the males.
The female Cooper's
Hawk does not hesitate to
hunt birds as large as Rock
Pigeons.

Look For

The Cooper's Hawk is slightly
larger and has a more rounded
tail tip than the similar-looking
Sharp-shinned Hawk, which is
also found in New Jersey.

Broad-winged Hawk
Buteo platypterus

The best time to see Broad-winged Hawks in New Jersey is during fall, when kettles of these buteos migrate south along interior ridges to wintering grounds in Central and South America. Hundreds or even thousands of these hawks take advantage of thermal air currents to soar, sometimes gliding for hours with barely a flap of the wing. • This shy hawk shuns open fields and forest clearings, preferring dense forests. In this habitat, its short, broad wings and highly flexible tail help it maneuver in the heavy growth.

Other ID: broad wings with pointed tips; dark brown upperparts. *Immature:* streaked underparts.
Size: L 14–19 in; W 32–39 in.
Voice: high-pitched, whistled *peeeo-wee-ee;* generally silent during migration.
Status: uncommon breeding species; fairly common fall migrant; uncommon in spring.
Habitat: *Breeding:* dense mixed and deciduous forests and woodlots. *In migration:* escarpments and shorelines; also uses riparian and deciduous forests and woodland edges.

Similar Birds

Red-shouldered Hawk

Red-tailed Hawk
(p. 78)

pale underwings
are outlined
with black

dark
"mustache"

light morph

heavily barred,
rufous brown
breast

light morph

Nesting: usually in a deciduous tree, often near water; bulky stick nest; usually builds a new nest each year; brown-spotted, whitish eggs are 2 x 1½ in; mostly the female incubates 2–4 eggs for 28–31 days; both adults raise the young.

Did You Know?

Of all the raptors, the Broad-winged Hawk is the most likely to be seen clutching a snake.

Look For

Most hunting is done from a high perch with a good view. When flushed, the Broad-winged Hawk will soon return to the same perch.

Red-tailed Hawk
Buteo jamaicensis

Take a midday drive through the country and look for Red-tailed Hawks soaring above the fields. Red-tails are the most commonly seen hawks in New Jersey and are found here year-round. • In milder weather, these hawks use thermals and updrafts to soar. The pockets of rising air provide substantial lift, which allows migrating hawks to fly for almost 2 miles without flapping their wings. On cooler days, resident Red-tails perch on exposed tree limbs, fence posts or utility poles to scan for prey.

Other ID: brown eyes; dark upperparts with white mottling on shoulders (scapulars). *Immature:* brownish tail. *In flight:* light underwing flight feathers with faint barring; fan-shaped tail.
Size: *Male:* L 18–23 in; W 4–5 ft.
Female: L 20–25 in; W 4–5 ft.
Voice: powerful, descending scream: *keeearrrr.*
Status: fairly common and widespread permanent resident; numbers are augmented in migration and winter.
Habitat: open country with some trees; also roadsides or woodlots.

Similar Birds

Rough-legged Hawk

Broad-winged Hawk
(p. 76)

Red-shouldered Hawk

dark shoulder patches

juvenile

dark leading edge on underside of wing

dark brown band of streaks across belly

red tail

Nesting: in woodlands adjacent to open habitat; bulky stick nest is enlarged each year; brown-blotched, whitish eggs are 2⅜ x 1⅞ in; pair incubates 2–4 eggs for 28–35 days.

Did You Know?

The Red-tailed Hawk's piercing call is often paired with the image of an eagle in TV commercials and movies.

Look For

Courting Red-tails will sometimes dive at one another, lock talons and tumble toward the earth, breaking away just before crashing into the ground.

American Kestrel
Falco sparverius

The colorful American Kestrel, formerly known as the "Sparrow Hawk," is a widespread falcon that is not shy of human activity and is adaptable to habitat change. This small falcon has benefited from the grassy rights-of-way created by interstate highways, which provide habitat for grasshoppers and other small prey. Unfortunately there have recently been substantial declines in its numbers. • Watch for this bird along rural roadways, perched on poles and telephone wires, or hovering over open country, foraging for insects and small mammals.

Other ID: 2 distinctive facial stripes; lightly spotted underparts; rusty barred back. *Male:* blue-gray crown with rusty cap. *In flight:* frequently hovers; buoyant, indirect flight style.
Size: L 7½–8 in; W 20–24 in.
Voice: usually silent; loud, often repeated, shrill *killy-killy-killy* when excited; female's voice is lower pitched.
Status: now a rare breeder; uncommon to fairly common migrant and winter visitor.
Habitat: open fields, woodlots, roadsides, grasslands and croplands.

Similar Birds

Merlin

Sharp-shinned Hawk
(p. 72)

Peregrine Falcon

long, rusty tail

rusty back
and wings

♀

blue-gray wings

♂

Nesting: in a tree cavity; may use a nest box; white to buff, brown-spotted eggs are 1½ x 1⅛ in; mostly the female incubates 4–6 eggs for 29–30 days; both adults raise the young.

Did You Know?

No stranger to captivity, the American Kestrel was the first falcon to reproduce by artificial insemination.

Look For

The kestrel often "wind-hovers" to scan the ground, flapping rapidly to maintain a stationary position while facing upwind.

Clapper Rail

Rallus longirostris

For years, Clapper Rail habitat throughout North America has been converted into airports, malls and landfills. As a result, these birds have been extirpated from many areas of the U.S.; in New Jersey, they can still be found in salt marshes at Forsythe (Brigantine) National Wildlife Refuge and at Cape May. • The eggs of Clapper Rails hatch over the course of a few days. Young rails leave the nest within hours of hatching, so adults often split up—one parent stays on the nest to incubate any remaining eggs, while the other moves to a nearby area where the hatchlings are safely brooded.

Other ID: long, slightly downcurved bill.
Size: *L* 14½ in; *W* 19 in.
Voice: call is a series of 10 or more loud, harsh *kek* notes, accelerating at first, then slowing toward the end; also a raspy, descending series of *whack* calls.
Status: fairly common permanent resident, but often stays hidden.
Habitat: tidal saltwater marshes of spartina (cordgrass); often feed along tidal channels during low tide.

Similar Birds

Virginia Rail

King Rail

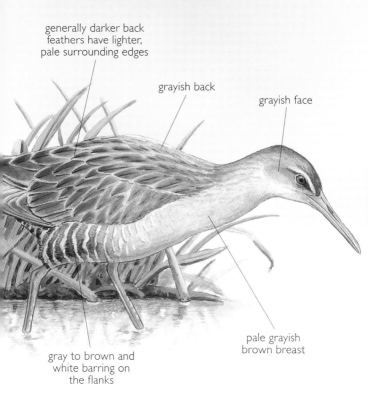

generally darker back
feathers have lighter,
pale surrounding edges

grayish back

grayish face

pale grayish
brown breast

gray to brown and
white barring on
the flanks

Nesting: in dense cover above or near water;
pair builds a cup nest of vegetation with a
domed canopy and an entrance ramp; pale,
sparsely spotted eggs are 1⅝ x 1¼ in; pair incubates 4–6 eggs for 20–24 days.

Did You Know?

One calling bird will often
cause an entire marsh to
erupt with the widely
scattered "chime-ins" of
other unseen rails.

Look For

The Clapper Rail characteris-
tically flicks its tail as it walks
and wades through tidal
marshes in search of crayfish,
crabs and other prey.

American Coot
Fulica americana

American Coots resemble ducks but are actually more closely related to rails and gallinules; they are the most widespread and abundant members of the rail family in North America. Only a few coots breed here yearly, but good numbers appear locally on our lakes and wetlands from September to May. • With feet that have individually webbed toes, the coot is adapted to diving, but it is just as likely to snatch a meal from other skilled divers whenever possible. • American Coots are also known as "Mud Hens."

Other ID: red eyes; long, yellow-green legs; lobed toes; small white marks on tail.
Size: *L* 13–16 in; *W* 24 in.
Voice: calls frequently in summer, day and night: *kuk-kuk-kuk-kuk-kuk;* also croaks and grunts.
Status: uncommon migrant and winter visitor; scarce and very local breeder.
Habitat: shallow marshes, ponds and wetlands with open water and emergent vegetation; sewage lagoons.

Similar Birds

Common Moorhen

Look For

Many features distinguish a coot from a duck, including head bobbing while swimming or walking and a narrower bill that extends up the forehead.

reddish spot on
white forehead
shield

gray-black overall

white, chicken-
like bill with
dark ring
around tip

Nesting: in emergent vegetation; pair builds
floating nest of cattails and grass; buffy white,
brown-spotted eggs are 2 x 1⅜ in; pair incubates 8–12 eggs for 21–25 days; double brooded.

Did You Know?

During spring, these birds are aggressive and territorial,
running along the surface of the water and charging intruders.
A confrontational coot will stab with its bill while trying to
grab the perpetrator with one clawed foot.

Black-bellied Plover
Pluvialis squatarola

Black-bellied Plovers may be seen along the coast during migration and winter, roosting in tight flocks or running along the mudflats when the tide goes out. They are usually found in coastal habitats but also occur in small numbers inland as migrants, near freshwater and in short-grass and dirt fields. Watch for small flocks flashing their bold, white wing stripes as they fly low over the water's surface. • Most plovers have three toes, but the Black-belly has a fourth toe higher on its leg, like most sandpipers.

Other ID: short, black bill; gray legs. *Breeding:* white stripe leads from crown down collar, neck and sides of breast; black face, breast, belly and flanks; white undertail coverts; black-and-white-mottled back. *In flight:* whitish tail.
Size: *L* 10½–13 in; *W* 29 in.
Voice: rich, plaintive, 3-syllable whistle: *pee-oo-ee,* usually given in flight.
Status: fairly common migrant and winter visitor along the coast; rare migrant inland.
Habitat: coastal mudflats, marshes and beaches; plowed fields and sod farms; the edges of lakeshores and reservoirs.

Similar Birds

American
Golden-Plover

Look For

The Black-bellied Plover may forage with the American Golden-Plover, an uncommon fall migrant that has a dark tail and lacks the dark "wing pits".

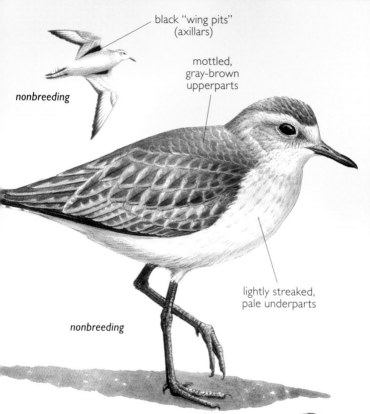

black "wing pits"
(axillars)

nonbreeding

mottled,
gray-brown
upperparts

lightly streaked,
pale underparts

nonbreeding

Nesting: does not nest in New Jersey; nests in the Arctic; hollow ground nest is lined with moss or lichen; darkly spotted, buff, greenish to grayish eggs are 2 x 1½ in; both adults incubate 3–4 eggs for 27 days.

Did You Know?

On the coast, these large plovers forage mostly at low or falling tide, often at night. They capture small invertebrates with a robinlike run-and-stop technique, frequently pausing to lift their heads for a reassuring scan of their surroundings.

Killdeer
Charadrius vociferus

The Killdeer is a gifted actor, well known for its "broken wing" distraction display. When an intruder wanders too close to its nest, the Killdeer greets the interloper with piteous cries while dragging a wing and stumbling about as if injured. Most predators take the bait and follow, and once the Killdeer has lured the predator far away from its nest, it miraculously recovers from its "injury" and flies off with a loud call.

Other ID: brown head; white neck band; brown back and upperwings; white underparts; rufous orange rump and base of tail. *Immature:* downy; only 1 breast band.
Size: *L* 9–11 in; *W* 24 in.
Voice: loud, distinctive *kill-dee kill-dee kill-deer;* variations include *deer-deer.*
Status: fairly common to common migrant; uncommon in summer and winter.
Habitat: open areas, such as fields, lakeshores, sandy beaches, mudflats, gravel streambeds, wet meadows and grasslands.

Similar Birds

Semipalmated Plover

Piping Plover

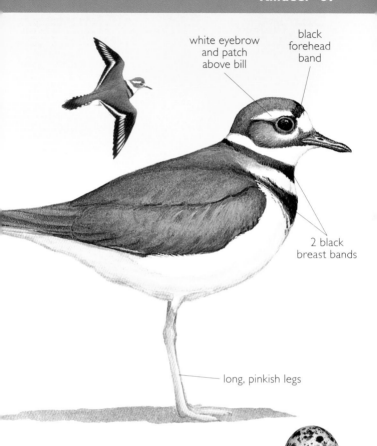

white eyebrow and patch above bill

black forehead band

2 black breast bands

long, pinkish legs

Nesting: on open ground, in a shallow, usually unlined depression; heavily marked, creamy buff eggs are 1⅜ x 1⅛ in; pair incubates 4 eggs for 24–28 days; may raise 2 broods.

Did You Know?

In spring, you might hear a European Starling imitate the vocal Killdeer's call.

Look For

The Killdeer has adapted well to urbanization, and it finds golf courses, farms, fields and abandoned industrial areas as much to its liking as shorelines.

American Oystercatcher

Haematopus palliatus

One of the few birds with a bill sturdy enough to pry open a mollusk shell, the American Oystercatcher eats a variety of shellfish, such as oysters, clams and mussels, as well as other intertidal invertebrates, including limpets, crabs, marine worms and even jellyfish.
• These large shorebirds usually forage alone or in pairs but form larger flocks during fall and winter.
• Oystercatchers can be found along the coast in central and southern New Jersey.

Other ID: short tail; stocky build. *Immature:* dark-tipped bill. *In flight:* bold white wing stripe and rump patch.
Size: L 18½ in; W 32 in.
Voice: call is a loud *wheet!*, often given in series during flight.
Status: fairly common in summer along the coast; winters only at a few locations, such as Brigantine Island and Stone Harbor Point.
Habitat: coastal marine habitats, including saltwater marshes, sandy beaches and tidal mudflats; will nest on dredge spoil islands.

Look For

During the spring and early-summer breeding season, watch for amusing courtship displays. These birds issue loud "piping" calls while they run along together side by side, bobbing their heads up and down. They may also take to the air, still calling and maintaining proximity.

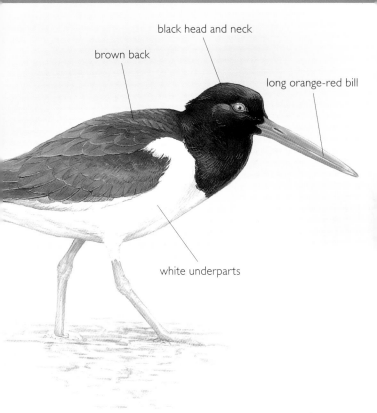

black head and neck

brown back

long orange-red bill

white underparts

Nesting: scrape nest in a sandy depression may be lined with dead plants, shells or pebbles; yellowish to brown, boldly marked eggs are 2¼ x 1½ in; both adults incubate 2–4 eggs for 24–27 days; may mate for life.

Did You Know?

American Oystercatchers may form a breeding trio, with two females and one male. Together, the group tends up to two nests and takes care of the young for the first few weeks. The downy hatchlings are able to leave the nest and forage for food a day or two after they are born.

Greater Yellowlegs
Tringa melanoleuca

The Greater Yellowlegs and Lesser Yellowlegs
(*T. flavipes*) are medium-sized sandpipers with
very similar plumages; they share the yellow legs
and feet that give them their English name. Both
species differ subtly, and a solitary yellowlegs
is difficult to identify until it flushes and
utters its distinctive call. The Greater Yellowlegs
peeps three times, whereas the Lesser Yellowlegs
peeps only once or twice and less stridently. As its
name suggests, the Greater Yellowlegs is the larger
species and has a longer, slightly upturned bill that
is about 1½ times the width of its head.

Other ID: plain plumage; bill may have a gray base.
Breeding: breast streaked; flanks barred with black.
Nonbreeding: upperparts less marked; dusky breast;
pale underparts. *In flight:* finely barred tail;
white rump.
Size: *L* 13–15 in; *W* 28 in.
Voice: call is a loud whistled *tew-tew-tew*.
Status: fairly common migrant; uncommon
winter visitor, primarily along the coast.
Habitat: any type of shallow wetland, whether
freshwater, brackish or saltwater; flooded agri-
cultural fields.

Similar Birds

Lesser Yellowlegs   Stilt Sandpiper   Wilson's Phalarope

finely streaked
head and neck

narrow, white
eye ring merges
with eye line

upperparts
speckled with
black and white

long, slightly
upturned bill
(longer than
length of head)

nonbreeding

long, yellow legs

nonbreeding

Nesting: does not breed in New Jersey; nests in northern and central Canada and Alaska; on the ground, near water; nest is a depression lined with leaves, moss and grass; darkly marked, pale creamy buff eggs are 2 x 1½ in; female incubates 4 eggs for 23 days.

Did You Know?

At the first sign of danger, the Greater Yellowlegs utters its loud, distinctive trisyllabic *tew-tew-tew* call to warn other shorebirds.

Look For

Shorebirds, including the Greater Yellowlegs, often stand or hop around beach-flats on one leg, a stance that conserves body heat.

Willet
Tringa semipalmata

Though plain and inconspicuous at rest, Willets
are striking in flight, revealing a bold black and
white pattern on their open wings. In late summer
and fall they are commonly found in flocks.
During the breeding season they utter loud *pill-
will-willet* calls. • There are two distinct subspecies
of the Willet, the western and the eastern. The
eastern race, *C. s. semipalmatus,* nests here and
rarely ventures far from the Atlantic Coast,
whereas the western race, *C. s. inornatus,* breeds
on the Great Plains, winters primarily along the
Pacific and Gulf coasts and occurs in small numbers in New Jersey during fall and winter.

Other ID: *Nonbreeding*: nondescript gray
upperparts; blackish bill with gray base; whitish
underparts. *In flight*: bold white wingstripe on
black wings.
Size: L 14–16 in; W 26 in.
Voice: call is a loud, rolling *pill-will willet.*
Status: fairly common breeder and migrant
along the coast; very rare inland and in winter.
Habitat: salt marshes, mudflats and beaches.

Similar Birds

Marbled Godwit

Greater Yellowlegs
(p. 92)

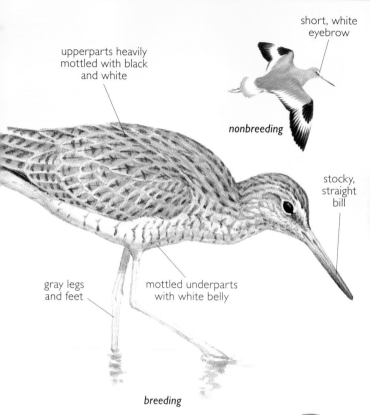

short, white
eyebrow

upperparts heavily
mottled with black
and white

nonbreeding

stocky,
straight
bill

gray legs
and feet

mottled underparts
with white belly

breeding

Nesting: scrapes out a depression in the sand
or mud; may be lined with vegetation; heavily
spotted, olive or buff eggs are 2¼ x 1½ in;
female incubates 4 eggs for 22 days.

Did You Know?

The Latin name *catop-
trophorus* means "mirror
bearing," referring to this
bird's white wing patches,
while *semipalmatus* means
"partially webbed feet."

Look For

When feeding, Willets often
spread out, but when one
bird takes flight, the entire
flock calls to each other and
follows suit.

Sanderling
Calidris alba

This pale shorebird graces sandy shorelines around the world. The Sanderling chases the waves in and out, snatching up aquatic invertebrates before they are swept back into the water. On shores where wave action is limited, it resorts to probing wet sand and mudflats for a meal of mollusks and insects. • To keep warm, Sanderlings seek the company of roosting sandpipers, plovers or turnstones and they often tuck one leg up while resting. Sanderlings often remain resolutely one-legged, hopping ahead of an advancing bench walker, evoking unnecessary concern.

Other ID: *Breeding:* dark mottling on rufous head, breast and upperparts.
Size: *L* 7–8½ in; *W* 17 in.
Voice: flight call is a sharp *kip* or *plick*.
Status: common migrant and winter visitor along the coast; rare migrant inland.
Habitat: sandy and muddy shorelines, cobble and pebble beaches, spits, lakeshores.

Similar Birds

Red Knot

Least Sandpiper
(p. 98)

Semipalmated Sandpiper

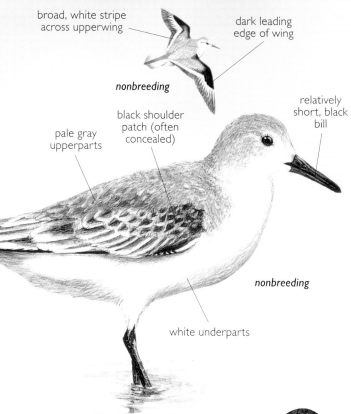

broad, white stripe across upperwing

dark leading edge of wing

nonbreeding

black shoulder patch (often concealed)

pale gray upperparts

relatively short, black bill

nonbreeding

white underparts

Nesting: does not nest in New Jersey; nests in the Arctic; on the ground; cup nest is lined with leaves; olive eggs, blotched with brown or purple are 1½ x 1 in; both sexes incubate 3–4 eggs for 23–24 days.

Did You Know?

The Sanderling is widespread, breeding across the Arctic and wintering on whatever continent it chooses, excluding Antarctica.

Look For

Sanderlings in pale, nonbreeding plumage have a ghostly glow as they forage at night on moonlit beaches.

Least Sandpiper
Calidris minutilla

The distinction of being the world's smallest shorebird doesn't make the Least Sandpiper any easier to identify. It falls into a confusing category of small, similar-looking sandpipers collectively known as "peeps." • To make the most of the brief arctic summer, female Least Sandpipers begin to develop their eggs as they migrate north. When they nest, the entire clutch may weigh more than half the weight of the female! The precocial young have only a few weeks to grow strong enough to endure their long migration southward.

Other ID: *Breeding:* buffy brown breast, head and nape. *Nonbreeding:* gray-brown head, nape and breast. *Juvenile:* resembles adult, but feathers of upperparts are richly patterned with dark centers and pale rusty edges.
Size: L 5–6½ in; W 13 in.
Voice: thin, high-pitched *kree-eep* or *kreeet* (the long e-tone is distinctive).
Status: fairly common migrant; very rare in winter.
Habitat: flooded fields, shallow sloughs and the shorelines of freshwater streams and lakes, salt marshes, mudflats and occasionally upper beaches.

Similar Birds

Semipalmated Sandpiper

Sanderling
(p. 96)

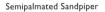

Western Sandpiper

breeding

dark-mottled back

short, dark bill often has pale base

light streaking on breast

nonbreeding

yellowish or greenish legs

Nesting: does not nest in New Jersey; nests in the Arctic and in taiga; on a tussock; in a shallow depression lined with vegetation; brown-blotched, pale buff eggs are 1¼ x ⅞ in; pair incubates 4 eggs for about 20 days.

Did You Know?

The Least Sandpiper migrates much of the length of the globe twice each year; some birds travel from the Arctic to South America and back again.

Look For

Unlike other peeps, Least Sandpipers rarely wade, preferring to feed on dry mud and use smaller wetlands.

Purple Sandpiper
Calidris maritima

The chunky Purple Sandpiper is an unusual shorebird in several respects. In the New World it is limited to North America—it does not winter in Central or South America. It is found in only the eastern half of North America—many shorebirds occur throughout the continent. Finally, it inhabits rocky shorelines, breakwaters and jetties, generally avoiding extensive beaches or mudflats.

• The Purple Sandpiper is one of our hardiest shorebirds, breeding in the Canadian Arctic and wintering along the Atlantic Coast. It expertly navigates its way across rugged, slippery rocks while foraging for crustaceans, mollusks and insect larvae.

Other ID: a medium-sized, dark, stocky shorebird. *Breeding:* very rarely seen in New Jersey; upperparts paler with some rufous wash; streaked head and breast.
Size: *L* 9 in; *W* 17 in.
Voice: call is a soft *prrt-prrt*.
Status: fairly common but somewhat local visitor from late fall to late spring.
Habitat: rocky shorelines, jetties and breakwaters; sometimes on beaches.

Similar Birds

Red Knot

Dunlin

dark gray upperparts
including head

thin, white
eye ring

nonbreeding

dark, slightly
downcurved bill
has a yellow-
orange base

white underparts
with scattered
dark streaking

orange legs
and feet

nonbreeding

Nesting: does not breed in New Jersey; nests on tundra in the eastern Arctic, Iceland and Greenland; scrape nest is lined with dead leaves; darkly marked, pale olive to bluish green eggs are 1½ x 1 in; both adults, but mainly male, incubate 3–4 eggs for 21–22 days.

Did You Know?

The name "purple" was given to this sandpiper for a purplish iridescence that is occasionally observed on its shoulders.

Look For

Small mixed flocks of Purple Sandpipers, Ruddy Turnstones and, sometimes, Sanderlings can be seen braving the surf breaking against the rocks.

Laughing Gull

Larus atricilla

Laughing Gulls were nearly extirpated from the Atlantic Coast in the late 19th century, when egg collecting was popular and feathers were in high demand for women's hats. East Coast populations have gradually recovered, and Laughing Gulls are once again common along our coastline. They loiter in parking lots, at fast-food restaurants and around beaches, and they often follow ferries, keeping a sharp eye out for human leftovers.

Other ID: *Nonbreeding:* white head with dark patch behind eye; black bill. *2nd-year:* white neck and underparts; dark gray back; black-tipped wings; black legs. *Immature:* variable plumage; brown to gray and white overall; broad, black subterminal tail band.

Size: *L* 15–17 in; *W* 3 ft.

Voice: loud, high-pitched, laughing call: *ha-ha-ha-ha-ha-ha.*

Status: common migrant and breeder along the Atlantic Coast and in Delaware Bay; common migrant along lower Delaware River, as well as some distance inland.

Habitat: primarily coastal, offshore in bays and estuaries; salt marshes and sandy beaches; also inland shores, streams, agricultural lands and landfills.

Similar Birds

Bonaparte's Gull   Little Gull

nonbreeding

black head

broken, white eye ring

red bill

breeding

Nesting: colonial nester; on dry islands, sandy coastal beaches or salt-marshes; builds a cup nest of marsh vegetation on the ground; brown, splotched eggs are 2¼ x 1½ in; both parents incubate 3 eggs for 22–27 days.

Did You Know?

Nesting colonies on small offshore islands and in salt marshes are vulnerable to spring storms and high tides that flood nests.

Look For

The Latin name *atricilla* refers to a black band present only on the tails of immature birds.

Ring-billed Gull
Larus delawarensis

Few people can claim that they have never seen these common and widespread gulls. Highly tolerant of humans, Ring-billed Gulls are part of our everyday lives, scavenging our litter and fouling our parks. These omnivorous gulls will eat almost anything and will swarm parks, beaches, golf courses and fast-food parking lots looking for food handouts. Though they often make pests of themselves, Ring-bills also help out farmers by following agricultural machinery to feast on many crop-destroying insects.

Other ID: *Nonbreeding:* dusky-streaked white head. *Immature:* brown in wings; strongly bicolored bill with pinkish base; pinkish legs. *In flight:* black wing tips with a few white spots.
Size: *L* 18–20 in; *W* 4 ft.
Voice: high-pitched *kakakaka-akakaka;* also a low, laughing *yook-yook-yook.*
Status: common migrant and winter visitor; a few nonbreeders stay the summer.
Habitat: nearshore ocean waters, lakes, rivers, coastlines of all types, landfills, golf courses, fields and parks.

Similar Birds

Herring Gull
(p. 106)

Iceland Gull

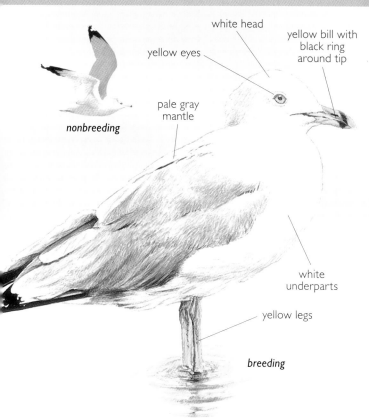

white head

yellow eyes

yellow bill with black ring around tip

pale gray mantle

nonbreeding

white underparts

yellow legs

breeding

Nesting: does not nest in New Jersey; nests in northern U.S. and Canada; colonial; in a shallow scrape on the ground lined with grasses, debris and small sticks; brown-blotched, gray to olive eggs are 2⅜ x 1⅝ in; pair incubates 2–4 eggs for 23–28 days.

Did You Know?

In chaotic nesting colonies, adult Ring-billed Gulls will call out and recognize the response of their chicks.

Look For

To differentiate between gulls, pay attention to their overall size, bill markings and the color of their backs, legs and eyes.

Herring Gull

Larus argentatus

These gulls are as skilled at scrounging handouts on the beach as their smaller Ring-billed relatives, but Herring Gulls are less numerous in urban settings. • When Herring Gulls arrive on their northern breeding grounds in spring, the landscape may still be covered in snow, but gulls can stand on ice for hours without freezing their feet. The arteries and veins in their legs run close together, so that blood flowing to the extremities warms the cooler blood traveling back to the core.

Other ID: yellow bill; light eyes; light gray mantle; white underparts. *Nonbreeding:* white head and nape are heavily streaked or mottled with brown. *Immature:* dark brown plumage lightens throughout the four years it takes to reach maturity.
Size: L 23–26 in; W 4 ft.
Voice: loud, buglelike *kleew-kleew;* also an alarmed *kak-kak-kak.*
Status: common permanent resident along the coast; common permanent nonbreeding resident inland; numbers are augmented in fall and winter.
Habitat: offshore waters, coastlines, large lakes, wetlands, rivers, landfills and urban areas.

Similar Birds

Ring-billed Gull
(p. 104)

Great Black-backed Gull
(p. 108)

nonbreeding

white head

red spot on
lower mandible

pink legs

breeding

Nesting: singly or colonially; on an open beach or island; in a shallow scrape lined with vegetation and sticks; darkly blotched, olive to buff eggs are 2¾ x 1⅞ in; pair incubates 3 eggs for 31–32 days.

Did You Know?

Nestlings use the small, red spot on the gull's lower bill as a target. A hungry chick will peck at the spot, cueing the parent to regurgitate its meal.

Look For

Although Herring Gulls are skilled hunters, they are opportunistic and can be seen scavenging on human leftovers in fast-food parking lots and landfills.

Great Black-backed Gull

Larus marinus

The Great Black-backed Gull's commanding size and slate gray mantle set it apart from other seabirds, but only adults have this distinctive plumage. For the first four years, immature gulls have dark streaking or mottling, which camouflages them from predators. • Like many marine gulls, Great Black-backed Gulls can drink salt water. Excess salt is removed from their bloodstream by tiny, specialized glands located above their eyes. The concentrated salty fluid then dribbles out of their nostrils.

Other ID: *Nonbreeding:* faintly streaked nape. *Immature:* mottled gray-brown, white and black; acquires dark back beginning in second winter; black or pale, black-tipped bill. *In flight:* white spots on wing tips.
Size: *L* 30 in; *W* 5½ ft.
Voice: a harsh *kyow*.
Status: common permanent resident along the coasts; common permanent nonbreeding resident on larger inland lakes and rivers; uncommon elsewhere.
Habitat: offshore ocean waters, coastlines, harbors, bays, landfills, large lakes and rivers.

Similar Birds

Lesser Black-backed Gull

Herring Gull
(p. 106)

slate gray mantle

yellow bill with red spot

breeding

pale pinkish legs

Nesting: usually colonial; on islands, cliff tops or beaches; pair builds a mound of vegetation and debris on the ground; brown-blotched, olive to buff eggs are 3 x 2⅛ in; pair incubates 2–3 eggs for 27–28 days.

Did You Know?

These opportunistic birds eat fish, eggs, invertebrates, small mammals and many birds. They also pirate food from other birds or scavenge at landfills.

Look For

A threatened gull will point its bill down, stretch out its neck and walk stiffly to warn away intruders.

Common Tern
Sterna hirundo

Common Terns are sleek, agile birds. They patrol coastal waters and the shorelines of lakes during spring and fall, settling in large, noisy nesting colonies during the summer months. • To win a mate, the male struts through the breeding colony with an offering of fish in his mouth. If a female accepts a suitor's gift, she pairs up with him to nest. • Parents defend their nest by diving repeatedly and aggressively at intruders, and they will even defecate on offenders to drive them away!

Other ID: *Nonbreeding:* white underparts; black nape; lacks black cap; black bar on shoulder.
In flight: shallowly forked tail; long, pointed wings; dark gray wedge near lighter gray upperwing tips.
Size: *L* 13–16 in; *W* 30 in.
Voice: high-pitched, drawn-out *keee-are;* most commonly heard at colonies but also in foraging flights.
Status: fairly common migrant and breeding species along the coast; very rare inland.
Habitat: coastal wetlands, nearshore ocean waters, islands and beaches.

Similar Birds

Forster's Tern   Least Tern   Caspian Tern

black cap

red bill with black tip

nonbreeding

white tail with gray outer edges

pale gray underparts

red legs

breeding

Nesting: colonial; on an island or upper beach; in a small scrape lined with pebbles, vegetation or shells; darkly blotched, creamy white eggs are 1⅝ x 1⅛ in; pair incubates 1–3 eggs for 20–24 days.

Did You Know?

Terns are effortless fliers and impressive long-distance migrants. Once, a Common Tern banded in Great Britain was recovered in Australia.

Look For

Terns hover over the water, then dive headfirst to capture small fish or aquatic invertebrates just below the surface.

Rock Pigeon
Columba livia

Colorful and familiar, the Rock Pigeon has an unusual feature: it feeds its young a substance similar to milk. This bird lacks mammary glands, but it produces a nutritious liquid, called "pigeon milk," in its crop. A chick inserts its bill down the adult's throat to reach the thick, protein-rich fluid. • This pigeon is likely a descendant of a Eurasian bird that was first domesticated about 4500 BC. European settlers introduced the Rock Pigeon to North America in the 17th century. Its tolerance of humans has made it a source of entertainment, as well as a pest.

Other ID: usually has orange feet. *In flight:* holds wings in a deep "V" while gliding; white rump on most birds.
Size: *L* 12–13 in; *W* 28 in (male is usually larger).
Voice: soft, cooing *coorrr-coorrr-coorrr.*
Status: common permanent resident.
Habitat: urban areas, railway yards and agricultural areas; high cliffs often provide more natural habitat.

Similar Birds

Mourning Dove
(p. 114)

Look For

No other "wild" bird varies as much in coloration. This variation is a result of years of semi-domestication and extensive inbreeding.

color is highly variable (iridescent blue-gray, red, white or tan)

white cere

Nesting: in a barn or on a cliff, bridge or tower; in a flimsy nest of sticks, grass and other vegetation; glossy white eggs are 1½ x 1⅛ in; pair incubates 2 eggs for 16–19 days; may raise broods year-round.

Did You Know?

Rock Pigeons have been used as food, as message couriers (both Caesar and Napoleon used them) and as scientific subjects. Much of our understanding of bird migration, endocrinology, sensory perception, flight and behavior derives from experiments involving these birds.

Mourning Dove

Zenaida macroura

The Mourning Dove's soft cooing, which filters through broken woodlands, farm country and suburban parks and yards, is often confused with the sound of a hooting owl. Beginning birders who track down the source of the calls are often surprised to find the streamlined silhouette of a perched dove. • This popular game animal is common throughout New Jersey and is one of the most abundant native birds in North America. Its numbers and range have increased since human development has created more open habitats and food sources, such as waste grain and bird feeders.

Other ID: buffy, gray-brown plumage; small head; dark bill; sleek body; dull red legs.
Size: *L* 11–13 in; *W* 18 in.
Voice: mournful, soft, slow *oh-woe-woe-woe*.
Status: common permanent resident; forms flocks in fall and winter.
Habitat: open woodlands, forest edges, agricultural and suburban areas and parks.

Similar Birds

Rock Pigeon
(p. 112)

Yellow-billed Cuckoo
(p. 116)

Black-billed Cuckoo

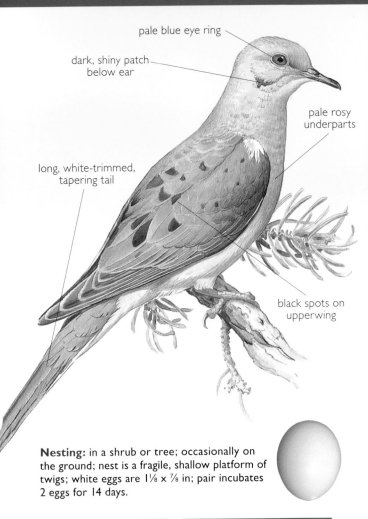

pale blue eye ring

dark, shiny patch
below ear

pale rosy
underparts

long, white-trimmed,
tapering tail

black spots on
upperwing

Nesting: in a shrub or tree; occasionally on the ground; nest is a fragile, shallow platform of twigs; white eggs are 1⅛ x ⅞ in; pair incubates 2 eggs for 14 days.

Did You Know?

In some parts of its range, the Mourning Dove may raise up to six broods each year—more than any other native bird.

Look For

When the Mourning Dove bursts into flight, its wings clap above and below its body. Its wings often create a whistling sound as it flies at high speed.

Yellow-billed Cuckoo

Coccyzus americanus

Large tracts of hardwood forest provide valuable habitat for the Yellow-billed Cuckoo, a bird that is declining over much of its range and has already disappeared in some states. The cuckoo's habitat has also steadily disappeared. • This bird skillfully negotiates its tangled home within impenetrable, deciduous undergrowth in silence, relying on obscurity for survival. Then, for a short period during nesting, the male cuckoo tempts fate by issuing a barrage of loud, rhythmic courtship calls. • Yellow-billed Cuckoos lay larger clutches when outbreaks of cicadas or tent caterpillars provide an abundant food supply.

Other ID: olive brown upperparts; white underparts.
Size: L 11–13 in; W 18 in.
Voice: long series of deep, hollow *kuks*, slowing near the end: *kuk-kuk-kuk-kuk kuk kop kow kowlp kowlp*.
Status: uncommon migrant and breeder.
Habitat: semi-open deciduous habitats; dense tangles and thickets at the edges of orchards and parks.

Similar Birds

Black-billed Cuckoo

Mourning Dove
(p. 114)

yellow
eye ring

rufous tinge
on primaries

mainly yellow,
slightly down-
curved bill with
black upper ridge

long tail with large
white spots on
underside

Nesting: on a low horizontal branch in a deciduous shrub or small tree; flimsy platform nest of twigs is lined with grass; pale bluish green eggs are 1¼ x ⅞ in; pair incubates 3–4 eggs for 9–11 days.

Did You Know?

Yellow-billed and Black-billed cuckoos, or "Rain Crows," have a propensity for calling on dark, cloudy days and a reputation for predicting rainstorms.

Look For

To find prey, the Yellow-billed Cuckoo often tries to flush insects from foliage by brushing its wings against the leaves.

Eastern Screech-Owl
Megascops asio

red morph

The diminutive Eastern Screech-Owl is a year-round resident of low-elevation, deciduous woodlands, but its presence is rarely detected—most screech-owls sleep away the daylight hours. • The noise of a mobbing horde of chickadees or a squawking gang of Blue Jays can alert you to an owl's presence during the day. Smaller birds that mob a screech-owl often do so after losing a family member during the night. • Screech-owls have one of the most varied diets of any owl and will capture small animals, earthworms, insects and even fish.

Other ID: reddish or grayish overall; yellow eyes; pale grayish bill.
Size: *L* 8–9 in; *W* 20–22 in.
Voice: horselike "whinny" that rises and falls.
Status: fairly common permanent resident.
Habitat: mature deciduous forests, open deciduous and riparian woodlands, orchards and shade trees with natural cavities.

Similar Birds

Northern
Saw-whet Owl

Look For

Eastern Screech-Owls—as well as mobbing landbirds—respond readily to whistled imitations of their calls.

short "ear" tufts

dark breast streaking

gray morph

Nesting: in an unlined natural cavity or artificial nest box; white eggs are 1½ x 1¼ in; female incubates 4–5 eggs for about 26 days; male brings food to the female during incubation.

Did You Know?

Eastern Screech-Owls are the only owls in New Jersey that show both red and gray color morphs. The gray morph is more common in our state. Very rarely, an intermediate brown morph occurs.

Great Horned Owl
Bubo virginianus

This highly adaptable and superbly camouflaged hunter has sharp hearing and powerful vision that allow it to hunt at night as well as by day. It will swoop down from a perch onto almost any small creature that moves. • An owl has specially designed feathers on its wings to reduce noise. The leading edge of the flight feathers is fringed rather than smooth, which interrupts airflow over the wing and allows the owl to fly silently. • Great Horned Owls begin their courtship as early as December or January, and by February and March the females are already incubating their eggs.

Other ID: dark brown overall with heavily mottled gray, brown and black upperparts; yellow eyes; white chin.
Size: L 18–25 in; W 3–5 ft.
Voice: breeding call is 4–6 deep hoots: *hoo-hoo-hoooo hoo-hoo* or *Who's awake? Me too;* female gives higher-pitched hoots.
Status: uncommon permanent resident.
Habitat: fragmented forests, fields, riparian woodlands, suburban parks and wooded edges of marshes.

Similar Birds

Long-eared Owl

Barred Owl

tall, widely spaced "ear" tufts form a triangle with beak

rusty orange facial disc is outlined in black

fine, horizontal barring on breast

Nesting: in another bird's abandoned stick nest or in a tree cavity; adds little or no nest material; dull whitish eggs are 2¼ x 1⅞ in; mostly the female incubates 2–3 eggs for 28–35 days.

Did You Know?

The Great Horned Owl has a poor sense of smell, which might explain why it is the only consistent predator of skunks.

Look For

Owls regurgitate pellets that contain the indigestible parts of their prey. You can find these pellets, which are generally clean and dry, under frequently used perches.

Chimney Swift

Chaetura pelagica

Chimney Swifts are the "frequent fliers" of the bird world—they feed, drink, bathe, collect nest material and even mate while they fly! They spend much of their time catching insects in the skies above New Jersey's towns and treetops. During night migrations, swifts sleep as they fly, relying on changing wind conditions to steer them. • Chimney Swifts have small, weak legs and cannot take flight again if they land on the ground. For this reason, swifts usually cling to vertical surfaces with their strong claws.

Other ID: gray-brown overall; pale throat; slim body. *In flight:* rapid wingbeats; boomerang-shaped profile; erratic flight pattern.
Size: *L* 5–5½ in; *W* 12–13 in.
Voice: call is a rapid chittering, given in flight; also gives a rapid series of staccato *chip* notes.
Status: fairly common migrant and breeder.
Habitat: forages above cities and towns; roosts and nests in chimneys; may nest in tree cavities in more remote areas.

Similar Birds

Northern Rough-winged Swallow

Bank Swallow

Barn Swallow
(p. 154)

long, thin, pointed, crescent-shaped wings

squared tail

Nesting: often colonial; half-saucer nest of short, dead twigs is attached to a vertical wall; white eggs are ¾ x ½ in; pair incubates 4–5 eggs for 19–21 days.

Did You Know?

Migrating Chimney Swifts may fly as high as 10,000 feet—above this altitude aircraft are required to carry oxygen.

Look For

In early evenings during migration, Chimney Swifts are often seen in large numbers swirling above large, old chimneys before they enter to roost for the night.

Ruby-throated Hummingbird

Archilochus colubris

Ruby-throated Hummingbirds feed on sweet, energy-rich flower nectar, pollinating flowers in the process. You can attract hummingbirds to your backyard with native, nectar-producing flowers such as pineapple sage, purple sage or bee balm, or with a nectar feeder filled with a sugarwater solution (red food coloring is both unnecessary and harmful to the birds). • Each year, these hummingbirds migrate across the Gulf of Mexico—a nonstop 500-mile journey—in spring and again in fall. They may lose up to one-third of their body mass while making this flight.

Other ID: pale underparts. *Female:* greenish gold crown and back. *Nonbreeding male:* dark brown to black throat. *Immature:* similar to female.
Size: L 3½–4 in; W 4–4½ in.
Voice: a soft *tew* and high squeaks; soft buzzing of the wings while in flight.
Status: uncommon migrant and breeder.
Habitat: open, mixed woodlands, orchards, tree-lined meadows, flower gardens and backyards with trees and feeders.

Look For

Hummingbirds are among the few bird species that can fly vertically and in reverse. When they hover, their unique, flexible wings move forward and backward, as if tracing a figure 8, rather than up and down.

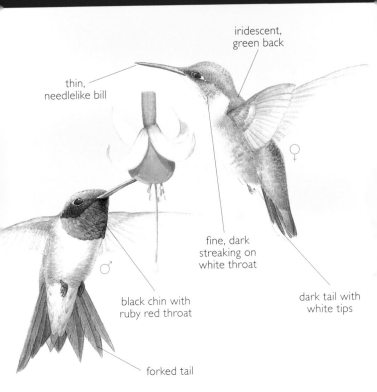

iridescent, green back

thin, needlelike bill

♀

fine, dark streaking on white throat

dark tail with white tips

black chin with ruby red throat

♂

forked tail

Nesting: on a horizontal tree limb; tiny, deep cup nest of plant down and fibers is held together with spider silk; lichens and leaves are pasted on the exterior walls; white eggs are ½ x ⅜ in; female incubates 2 eggs for 13–16 days.

Did You Know?

Weighing about as much as a nickel, a hummingbird can briefly reach speeds of up to 60 miles per hour. In straight-ahead flight, hummingbirds beat their wings up to 80 times per second, and their hearts can beat up to 1200 times per minute!

Belted Kingfisher
Ceryle alcyon

Perched on a bare branch over a productive pool or stream, the Belted Kingfisher utters a scratchy, rattling call. Then, with little regard for its scruffy hairdo, it plunges headfirst into the water, snatching a fish or a frog. Back on land, the kingfisher flips its prey into the air and swallows it headfirst. Similar to owls, kingfishers regurgitate the indigestible portion of their food as pellets, which can be found beneath favorite perches. • Nestlings have closed eyes and are featherless for the first week, but after five days they are able to swallow small fish whole.

Other ID: bluish upperparts; small white patch near eye; straight bill; short legs; white underwings.
Size: L 11–14 in; W 20–21 in.
Voice: fast, repetitive, cackling rattle, like a teacup shaking on a saucer.
Status: uncommon breeder; numbers are augmented in fall and winter.
Habitat: rivers, large streams, lakes, marshes and beaver ponds, especially near exposed soil banks, gravel pits or bluffs.

Similar Birds

Blue Jay
(p. 144)

Look For

With an extra red band across her belly, the female kingfisher is more colorful than her mate, an uncommon trait for female birds.

shaggy crest

white collar

♀

♂

blue-gray
breast band

rust-colored belt
on female may be
incomplete

Nesting: in a cavity at the end of an earth
burrow; glossy white eggs are 1⅜ x 1 in; pair
incubates 6–7 eggs for 22–24 days.

Did You Know?

In Greek mythology, Alcyon, the daughter of the wind god,
grieved so deeply for her drowned husband that the gods
transformed them both into kingfishers.

Red-bellied Woodpecker

Melanerpes carolinus

The familiar Red-bellied Woodpecker is no stranger to suburban backyards and deciduous woodlands and will sometimes nest in birdhouses. This widespread bird is found year-round throughout the eastern states. • Unlike most woodpeckers, Red-bellies consume large amounts of plant material, seldom excavating wood for insects. • When occupying an area together with Red-headed Woodpeckers, Red-bellies will nest in the trunk, below the foliage, and the Red-heads will nest in dead branches among the foliage.

Other ID: orange-red tinge on belly is difficult to see.
Size: *L* 9–10½ in; *W* 16 in.
Voice: call is a soft, rolling *churr*; drums in second-long bursts.
Status: common permanent resident.
Habitat: mature deciduous woodlands; wooded residential areas; often visits feeders, particularly in winter.

Similar Birds

Northern Flicker
(p. 132)

Red-headed
Woodpecker

black and white
barring on back

red nape
extends to
forehead

♂

red nape

♀

white patches on
rump are speckled
with black

Nesting: nests in woodlands and residential
areas; in a cavity excavated mainly by the male;
white eggs are 1 x ¾ in; pair incubates 4–5 eggs
for 12–14 days; both adults raise the young.

Did You Know?

Studies of banded Red-
bellied Woodpeckers have
shown that these birds
have a life span in the wild
of more than 20 years.

Look For

The Red-bellied Woodpecker's
namesake, its red belly, is only
a small reddish area that is
difficult to see in the field.

Downy Woodpecker

Picoides pubescens

A bird feeder well stocked with peanut butter, suet or black-oil sunflower seeds may attract a pair of Downy Woodpeckers to your backyard. These approachable little birds are more tolerant of human activity than most other woodpecker species, and they visit feeders more often than the larger, more aggressive Hairy Woodpeckers (*P. villosus*). • Like other woodpeckers, the Downy has evolved special features to help cushion the shock of repeated hammering, including a strong bill and neck muscles, a flexible, reinforced skull and a brain that is tightly packed in its protective cranium.

Other ID: black eye line and crown; white belly; broad white stripe on back. *Male:* small, red patch on back of head. *Female:* no red patch.
Size: L 6–7 in; W 12 in.
Voice: long, unbroken trill; calls are a sharp *pik* or *ki-ki-ki* or a whiny *queek queek*.
Status: common permanent resident.
Habitat: any wooded environment, especially deciduous and mixed forests and areas with tall, deciduous shrubs.

Similar Birds

Hairy Woodpecker

Yellow-bellied
Sapsucker

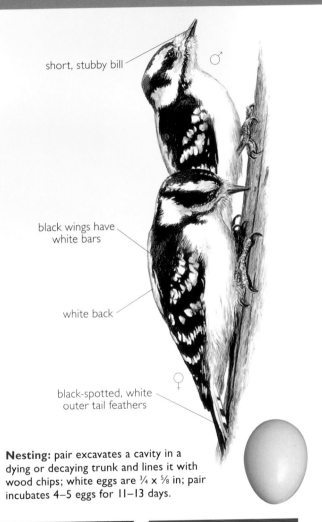

short, stubby bill

♂

black wings have white bars

white back

♀

black-spotted, white outer tail feathers

Nesting: pair excavates a cavity in a dying or decaying trunk and lines it with wood chips; white eggs are ¾ x ⅝ in; pair incubates 4–5 eggs for 11–13 days.

Did You Know?

Woodpeckers have feathered nostrils, which filter out the sawdust produced by hammering.

Look For

The Downy Woodpecker uses its small bill to probe tiny crevices for invertebrates and wood-boring grubs.

Northern Flicker
Colaptes auratus

Instead of boring holes in trees, the Northern Flicker scours the ground in search of invertebrates, particularly ants. With robinlike hops, it investigates anthills, grassy meadows and forest clearings. • Flickers often bathe in dusty depressions. The dust particles absorb oils and bacteria that can harm the birds' feathers. To clean themselves even more thoroughly, flickers squash ants and preen themselves with the remains. Ants contain formic acid, which kills small parasites on the birds' skin and feathers.

Other ID: long bill; gray crown; white rump. *Male:* black "mustache." *Female:* no "mustache."
Size: L 12–13 in; W 20 in.
Voice: loud, "laughing," rapid *kick-kick-kick-kick-kick-kick*; *woika-woika-woika* issued during courtship.
Status: fairly common nesting species; common in migration; uncommon in winter.
Habitat: open woodlands and forest edges, fields, meadows, beaver ponds and suburban parks and yards.

Similar Birds

Red-bellied Woodpecker (p. 128)

Yellow-bellied Sapsucker

barred, brown
back and wings

♂

brownish
cheeks

black-spotted,
buff to whitish
underparts

red nape
crescent

black "bib"

♀

yellow underwings
and undertail

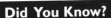

Nesting: pair excavates a cavity in a dying or decaying trunk and lines it with wood chips; may also use a nest box; white eggs are 1⅛ x ⅞ in; pair incubates 5–8 eggs for 11–16 days.

Did You Know?

The very long tongue of a woodpecker wraps around twin structures in the skull and is stored in much the same way as a measuring tape is stored in its case.

Look For

Many woodpeckers have zygodactyl feet—two toes point forward and two point back—which allows them to move vertically up and down tree trunks.

Eastern Wood-Pewee
Contopus virens

Our most common and widespread woodland fly-catcher, the Eastern Wood-Pewee, breeds in every county in New Jersey. The male is readily detected by his plaintive song, which is repeated throughout much of the day during late spring and early summer. Some of the keenest suitors will even sing late into the evening. • Many insects have evolved defense mechanisms to avert potential predators such as the Eastern Wood-Pewee and its flycatching relatives.

Other ID: slender body; whitish throat; gray breast and sides.
Size: *L* 6–6½ in; *W* 10 in.
Voice: *Male:* song is a clear, slow, plaintive *pee-ah-wee*, with the 2nd note lower, followed by a downslurred *pee-oh*, with or without intermittent pauses; also a *chip* call.
Status: uncommon to fairly common migrant and breeder.
Habitat: open mixed and deciduous woodlands with a sparse understory, especially woodland openings and edges; rarely in open coniferous woodlands.

Similar Birds

Willow Flycatcher

Least Flycatcher

Eastern Phoebe
(p. 136)

dark face with
weak eye ring

olive gray to olive
brown upperparts

2-toned bill is
dark above and
dull yellow-
orange below

2 narrow, white
wing bars

whitish or pale
yellow belly, flanks and
undertail coverts

long wings

Nesting: on the fork of a horizontal deciduous branch, well away from the trunk; open cup of plants and lichen is bound with spider silk; whitish, darkly blotched eggs are 1¹⁄₁₆ x ⁹⁄₁₆ in; female incubates 3 eggs for 12–13 days.

Did You Know?

Sometimes you can hear the snap of a wood-pewee's bill closing around an insect.

Look For

Like other flycatchers, the Eastern Wood-Pewee loops out from exposed perches to snatch flying insects in midair, a technique often referred to as "flycatching" or "hawking."

Eastern Phoebe
Sayornis phoebe

Whether you are poking around a small bridge, barnyard, campground picnic shelter or your backyard shed, there is a chance you will stumble upon an Eastern Phoebe family and their marvelous mud nest. The Eastern Phoebe's nest building and territorial defense are normally well underway by the time most other songbirds arrive in New Jersey in mid-May. Once limited to nesting on natural cliffs and fallen riparian trees, this adaptive flycatcher can now be found nesting in culverts and under bridges and eaves, especially when water is near.

Other ID: gray-brown upperparts; belly may be washed with yellow in fall; no eye ring; weak wing bars; dark legs and bill.
Size: L 6½–7 in; W 10½ in.
Voice: *Male:* song is a hearty, snappy *fee-bee*, delivered frequently; call is a sharp *chip*.
Status: uncommon to fairly common spring migrant and breeder; fairly common in fall; rare in early winter in southern New Jersey.
Habitat: open deciduous woodlands, overgrown fields, forest edges and clearings; often near water.

Similar Birds

Eastern Wood-Pewee
(p. 134)

Willow Flycatcher

Eastern Kingbird
(p. 140)

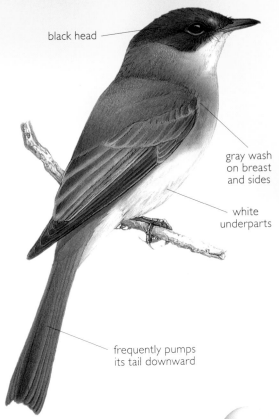

black head

gray wash
on breast
and sides

white
underparts

frequently pumps
its tail downward

Nesting: under the ledge of a building, picnic shelter, culvert, bridge, cliff or well; cup-shaped mud nest is lined with soft material; white, red-spotted eggs are ¾ x ⁹⁄₁₆ in; female incubates 4–5 eggs for about 16 days.

Did You Know?

Eastern Phoebes sometimes reuse their nest sites for many years. Females save energy this way and are often able to lay more eggs.

Look For

Some other birds pump their tails while perched, but few species can match the zest and frequency of the Eastern Phoebe's tail pumping.

Great Crested Flycatcher

Myiarchus crinitus

Loud, raucous calls give away the presence of the brightly colored Great Crested Flycatcher. This large flycatcher often inhabits forest edges and nests in woodlands throughout New Jersey. Unlike other eastern flycatchers, the Great Crested prefers to nest in a tree cavity or abandoned woodpecker hole, or sometimes uses a nest box intended for a bluebird. Once in a while, the Great Crested Flycatcher will decorate the nest entrance with a shed snakeskin or a piece of translucent plastic wrap. The purpose of this practice is not fully understood, though it might make any would-be predators think twice.

Other ID: dark olive brown upperparts; thick, black bill with pale base.
Size: L 8–9 in; W 13 in.
Voice: loud, whistled *wheep!* and a rolling *prrrrreet!*
Status: fairly common migrant and breeder.
Habitat: deciduous and mixed woodlands and forests, usually near openings or edges.

Similar Birds

Eastern Phoebe
(p. 136)

Western Kingbird

peaked head

rufous brown
wings and tail

gray throat and
upper breast

bright yellow belly
and undertail coverts

Nesting: in a tree cavity or nest box; nest is lined with soft material; may hang a shed snake-skin from the entrance hole; heavily marked, creamy white to pale buff eggs are ⅞ x ⅝ in; female incubates 5 eggs for 13–15 days.

Did You Know?

Many animals depend on tree cavities for shelter and nesting, so instead of cutting down large, dead trees, consider leaving a few standing.

Look For

Follow the loud *wheep!* calls and watch for a show of bright yellow and rufous feathers to find this fly-catcher.

Eastern Kingbird
Tyrannus tyrannus

Sometimes referred to as the "Jekyll and Hyde" bird, the Eastern Kingbird is a gregarious fruit eater while wintering in South America, and an antisocial, aggressive insect eater while nesting in North America. • The Eastern Kingbird fearlessly attacks crows and hawks that pass through its territory, pursuing and pecking at them until the threat has passed. No one familiar with the Eastern Kingbird's pugnacious behavior will refute its scientific name, *Tyrannus tyrannus*. • This bird reveals a gentler side of its character in its quivering, butterfly-like courtship flight.

Other ID: black bill; no eye ring; white underparts; light grayish wash on breast; dark legs.
Size: *L* 8½–9 in; *W* 15 in.
Voice: call is a quick, loud, chattering *kit-kit-kitter-kitter;* also a buzzy *dzee-dzee-dzee.*
Status: common migrant and breeder.
Habitat: fields with scattered shrubs, trees or hedgerows; forest fringes, clearings, shrubby roadsides, towns and farmyards.

Similar Birds

Eastern Wood-Pewee
(p. 134)

Olive-sided Flycatcher

Tree Swallow
(p. 152)

small head crest

thin, orange-red crown
(very rarely seen)

dark gray to black
upperparts

white-tipped tail

Nesting: on a horizontal limb, stump or upturned tree root; cup nest is made of weeds, twigs and grass; darkly blotched, white to pinkish white eggs are 1 x ¾ in; female incubates 3–4 eggs for 14–18 days.

Did You Know?

Eastern Kingbirds rarely walk or hop on the ground—they prefer to fly, even for very short distances.

Look For

Eastern Kingbirds are common and widespread. On a drive in the country you will likely spot at least one of these birds sitting on a fence or utility wire.

Red-eyed Vireo

Vireo olivaceus

Capable of delivering about 40 phrases per minute, the male Red-eyed Vireo can out-sing any one of his courting neighbors. One tenacious male set a record by singing 21,000 phrases in one day! • Although you may still hear the Red-eyed Vireo singing five or six hours after other songbirds have ceased for the day, this bird is not easy to spot. Its olive and white plumage usually blends in with the foliage of deciduous trees and its unique red eyes, unusual among songbirds, are even trickier to spot without a good pair of binoculars.

Other ID: olive cheek; olive green upperparts; white to pale gray underparts.
Size: L 6 in; W 10 in.
Voice: call is a short, scolding *rreeah. Male:* song is a series of quick, continuous, variable phrases with pauses in between: *look-up, way-up, tree-top, see-me, here-I-am!*
Status: fairly common to common breeder and migrant.
Habitat: deciduous or mixed woodlands.

Similar Birds

Warbling Vireo

Tennessee Warbler

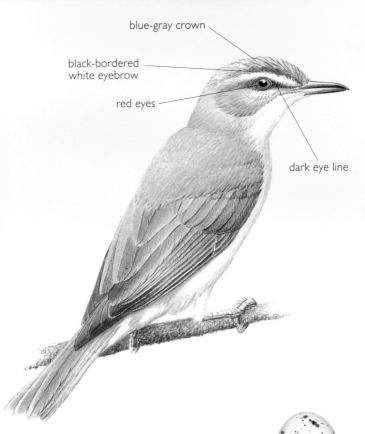

blue-gray crown

black-bordered
white eyebrow

red eyes

dark eye line

Nesting: in a tree; hanging cup nest is made of grass, roots, spider silk and cocoons; darkly spotted, white eggs are ¾ x ½ in; female incubates 4 eggs for 11–14 days.

Did You Know?

If a Brown-headed Cowbird parasitizes its nest, a Red-eyed Vireo will either abandon the nest or raise the cowbird young with its own.

Look For

The Red-eyed Vireo perches with a hunched stance and hops with its body turned diagonally to its direction of travel.

Blue Jay

Cyanocitta cristata

The Blue Jay is the only blue member of the corvid family in New Jersey. White-flecked wing feathers and sharply defined facial features make this bird easy to recognize. • Jays can be quite aggressive when competing for sunflower seeds and peanuts at backyard feeding stations and rarely hesitate to drive away smaller birds, squirrels or threatening cats. Even the Great Horned Owl is not too formidable a predator for a group of these brave, boisterous mobsters to harass.

Other ID: blue upperparts; white underparts; black bill.

Size: *L* 11–12 in; *W* 16 in.

Voice: noisy, screaming *jay-jay-jay*; nasal *queedle queedle queedle-queedle* sounds like a muted trumpet; often imitates various sounds, including calls of other birds.

Status: common permanent resident; migrants from farther north may be seen in fall, winter and spring.

Habitat: mixed deciduous forests, agricultural areas, scrubby fields, yards and feeders.

Similar Birds

Belted Kingfisher
(p. 126)

Eastern Bluebird
(p. 168)

blue crest

white bars
and flecking
on the wings

black "necklace"

blue tail with dark
bars and white
corners

Nesting: in a tree or tall shrub; pair builds
a bulky stick nest; greenish, buff or pale eggs,
spotted with gray and brown, are 1⅛ x ¾ in;
pair incubates 4–5 eggs for 16–18 days.

Did You Know?

The Blue Jay can imitate
the call of a Red-tailed
Hawk, American Crow or
even a neighborhood cat
with uncanny accuracy.

Look For

Blue Jays store food from
feeders in trees and other
places for later use.

American Crow

Corvus brachyrhynchos

The noise that most often emanates from this treetop squawker seems unrepresentative of its intelligence. However, this wary, clever bird is also an impressive mimic, able to whine like a dog and laugh or cry like a human. • American Crows have flourished in spite of considerable efforts, over many generations, to reduce their numbers. As ecological generalists, crows can survive in a wide variety of habitats and conditions. In January, when crows in the southern U.S. are busy capturing frogs and lizards in thriving wetlands, crows in more northerly locales are searching snow-covered fields for mice or carrion.

Other ID: glossy, purple-black plumage; black bill and legs.
Size: *L* 17–21 in; *W* 3 ft.
Voice: distinctive, far-carrying, repetitive *caw-caw-caw.*
Status: common permanent resident; may form large winter roosts.
Habitat: urban and residential areas, agricultural fields and other open areas with scattered woodlands.

Similar Birds

Fish Crow
(p. 148)

Common Raven

Common Grackle
(p. 218)

short, square-shaped tail

slim, sleek head
and throat

Nesting: in a tree or on a utility pole; large stick-and-branch nest is lined with fur and soft plant materials; darkly blotched, gray-green to blue-green eggs are 1⅝ x 1⅛ in; female incubates 4–6 eggs for about 18 days.

Did You Know?

Crows are family oriented, and the young from the previous year may help their parents raise the nestlings.

Look For

Crows will often drop walnuts or clams from great heights onto a hard surface to crack the shells, one of the few examples of birds using objects to manipulate food.

Fish Crow
Corvus ossifragus

Although Fish Crows and American Crows are
virtually identical in plumage, their habitat and
call notes readily separate the two species. The
common call of a Fish Crow is an *uh* or *uh-uh*,
whereas the common call of an American Crow is
a raucous *caw!* It is not known whether competition or habitat preferences segregate our two crow
species, but they usually occur together only at
winter roosts. • The Fish Crow is a coastal species
found only in the eastern United States, from New
Hampshire to Texas. It occurs in coastal habitats
of central and southern New Jersey and appears
to be extending its range northward.

Other ID: virtually identical to American Crow,
but averages slightly smaller; best identified by
voice.
Size: *L* 15 in; *W* 3 ft.
Voice: common call is a nasal *uh* or *uh-uh*;
juvenile American Crows may sound nasal as
well but do not give the 2-note *uh-uh*.
Status: fairly common permanent resident;
may form localized flocks in winter.
Habitat: urban and suburban areas including
landfills; marshes, coastlines and along inland
lakes and rivers.

Similar Birds

American Crow
(p. 146)

Common Raven

glossy black plumage

small head and sleek throat

short legs

Nesting: in a tree; often in small, loose colonies; both sexes build a bulky nest of sticks; heavily marked, greenish eggs are 1½ x 1 in; female incubates 4–5 eggs for 16–18 days.

Did You Know?

Highly social, corvids are among the most clever birds. They have superb memories and are able to learn, make simple tools and problem solve.

Look For

Watch for Fish Crows in coastal areas, American Crows in suburbs and larger, thick-billed Common Ravens in northwestern New Jersey highlands.

Purple Martin

Progne subis

If you set up "condo complexes" for them, these large swallows will entertain you throughout spring and summer. You can watch martin adults spiral around their accommodations in pursuit of flying insects, while their young perch clumsily at the cavity openings. Purple Martins once nested in natural tree hollows and in cliff crevices but have virtually abandoned these in favor of human-made housing. • To prevent the invasion of aggressive House Sparrows or European Starlings, it is essential to clean out and close up martin condos after each nesting season.

Other ID: pointed wings; small bill. *Female and immature:* blue-brown upperparts with gray collar; sooty gray underparts.
Size: *L* 7–8 in; *W* 18 in.
Voice: rich, fluty, robinlike *pew-pew*, often heard in flight.
Status: uncommon to fairly common but local breeder, usually near martin houses; 1 or 2 huge aggregations of thousands of birds form in late summer on Delaware Bayshore.
Habitat: semi-open areas, often near water.

Similar Birds

European Starling
(p. 182)

Bank Swallow

Northern Rough-
winged Swallow

glossy, dark
blue body

slightly
forked tail

dark underparts

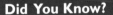

Nesting: communal; in a human-made bird-house or hollowed-out gourd; nest is made of feathers, grass and mud; white eggs are 1 x ⅝ in; female incubates 4–5 eggs for 15–18 days.

Did You Know?

The Purple Martin is North America's largest swallow.

Look For

Purple Martins are attracted to martin condo complexes erected in open areas, high on a pole and near a body of water.

Tree Swallow
Tachycineta bicolor

The Tree Swallow, one of our most common summer swallow species, is often seen perched beside its fence post nest box. • When conditions are favorable, these busy birds are known to return to their young 10 to 20 times per hour (about 140 to 300 times a day!). This nearly ceaseless activity provides observers with plenty of opportunities to watch and photograph these birds in action. • In the evening and during light rains, small groups of foraging Tree Swallows sail gracefully above rivers, ponds and wetlands, catching stoneflies, mayflies and caddisflies.

Other ID: white underparts; no white on cheek. *Female:* slightly duller. *Immature:* brown upperparts; white underparts; dusky band on breast. *In flight:* long, pointed wings.
Size: L 5½ in; W 14½ in.
Voice: alarm call is a metallic, buzzy *klweet*. *Male:* song is a liquid, chattering twitter.
Status: common breeder and migrant; rare in winter in south coastal New Jersey.
Habitat: open areas; fencelines with bluebird nest boxes and fringes of open woodlands, especially near water.

Similar Birds

Eastern Kingbird
(p. 140)

Bank Swallow

Northern Rough-winged Swallow

iridescent, dark blue or blue-green head and upperparts

small bill

shallowly forked tail

Nesting: in a tree cavity or nest box lined with weeds, grass and feathers; white eggs are ¾ x ½ in; female incubates 4–6 eggs for up to 19 days.

Did You Know?

Between August and November, huge flocks of Tree Swallows may congregate over coastal marshes, sometimes numbering over 10,000 birds.

Look For

In the bright sunshine, the Tree Swallow's back appears blue; prior to fall migration the back appears green.

Barn Swallow
Hirundo rustica

When you encounter this bird, you might first notice its distinctive, deeply forked tail—or you might just find yourself repeatedly ducking to avoid the dives of a protective parent. • Barn Swallows once nested on cliffs, but they are now found more frequently nesting inside barns, boathouses and under bridges and house eaves. The messy young and aggressive parents unfortunately often motivate people to remove nests just as nesting season is beginning, but this bird's close association with humans allows us to observe the normally secretive reproductive cycle of birds.

Other ID: blue-black upperparts; long, pointed wings.
Size: L 7 in; W 15 in.
Voice: continuous, twittering chatter: *zip-zip-zip* or *kvick-kvick.*
Status: common breeder and migrant.
Habitat: open rural and suburban areas where bridges, culverts and buildings are found near water.

Similar Birds

Cliff Swallow

Northern Rough-
winged Swallow

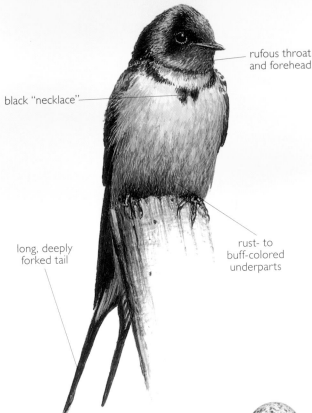

rufous throat and forehead

black "necklace"

rust- to buff-colored underparts

long, deeply forked tail

Nesting: singly or in small, loose colonies; on a human-made structure under an overhang; half- or full-cup nest is made of mud, grass and straw; brown-spotted, white eggs are ¾ x ½ in; pair incubates 4–7 eggs for 13–17 days.

Did You Know?

The Barn Swallow is a natural pest controller, feeding on insects that are often harmful to crops and livestock.

Look For

Barn Swallows roll mud into small balls and build their nests one mouthful of mud at a time.

Carolina Chickadee
Poecile carolinensis

Fidgety, friendly Carolina Chickadees are familiar to anyone in southern New Jersey with a backyard feeder well stocked with sunflower seeds and peanut butter. These agile birds even hang upside down to grab insects and pluck berries. Like some woodpeckers and nuthatches, the Carolina Chickadee will hoard food for later in the season when food may become scarce. • It's hard to imagine a chickadee using its tiny bill to excavate a nesting cavity, but come breeding season, this energetic little bird can be found hammering out a hollow in a rotting tree.

Other ID: black "bib"; white cheeks; white underparts; buffy flanks.
Size: L 4¾ in; W 7½ in.
Voice: whistling song has 4 clear notes sounding like *fee-bee fee-bay.*
Status: common permanent resident south of the Raritan River.
Habitat: deciduous and mixed woods, riparian woodlands, groves and isolated shade trees; frequents suburban areas and feeders.

Similar Birds

Black-capped Chickadee
(p. 158)

White-breasted
Nuthatch (p. 162)

black cap

grayish nape

gray upperparts
and secondaries

Nesting: excavates or enlarges a tree cavity;
may also use a nest box; cavity is lined with
soft material; white eggs, marked with reddish
brown, are $9/16$ x $7/16$ in; female incubates 5–8 eggs
for 11–14 days.

Did You Know?

Chickadee flocks are
often made up of close
family members that vig-
orously defend the same
territory for many generations.

Look For

Outside of the breeding season, chickadees often forage
in mixed-species flocks with
titmice, vireos, warblers,
kinglets, nuthatches, creepers
and small woodpeckers.

Black-capped Chickadee
Poecile atricapillus

You can catch a glimpse of this incredibly sociable chickadee in northern New Jersey at any time of the year. In winter, Black-cappeds join kinglets, nuthatches, creepers and small woodpeckers; in spring and fall, they may join mixed flocks of vireos and warblers. • You may be able to entice a Black-capped Chickadee to the palm of your hand with the help of a sunflower seed.

Other ID: black "bib"; white underparts; light buff sides and flanks; dark legs.
Size: *L* 5–6 in; *W* 8 in.
Voice: call is a chipper, whistled *chick-a-dee-dee dee;* song is a slow, whistled *swee-tee* or *fee-bee.*
Status: common permanent resident north of the Raritan River; a few birds wander slightly south in winter, sometimes overlaps with the Carolina Chickadee; a few records of hybrids are known from the central part of the state.
Habitat: deciduous and mixed forests, riparian woodlands and suburban neighborhoods.

Similar Birds

Carolina Chickadee
(p. 156)

Look For

Chickadees store food in holes and bark crevices or anywhere it will be easy to locate when needed.

black cap

white cheek

gray back
and wings

white edging on
wing feathers

Nesting: pair excavates a cavity in a rotting tree or stump, or occasionally uses a birdhouse; cavity is lined with fur, feathers, moss, grass and cocoons; finely speckled, white eggs are ⅝ x ½ in; female incubates 6–8 eggs for 12–13 days.

Did You Know?

On cold nights, chickadees enter into a hypothermic state, lowering their body temperature and heartbeat considerably to conserve energy.

Tufted Titmouse
Baeolophus bicolor

This bird's amusing feeding antics and insatiable appetite keep curious observers entertained at bird feeders. Grasping a sunflower seed with its tiny feet, the dexterous Tufted Titmouse will strike its dainty bill repeatedly against the hard outer coating to expose the inner core. • A breeding pair of Tufted Titmice will maintain their bond throughout the year, even when joining small, mixed-species flocks for the cold winter months. The titmouse family bond is so strong that the young from one breeding season will often stay with their parents long enough to help them with nesting and feeding duties the following year.

Other ID: white underparts; pale face.
Size: L 6–6½ in; W 10 in.
Voice: noisy, scolding call, like that of a chickadee; song is a whistled *peter peter* or *peter peter peter.*
Status: common permanent resident; largely nonmigratory.
Habitat: deciduous woodlands, groves and suburban parks; neighborhoods with large, mature trees or backyard feeders.

Similar Birds

Black-capped Chickadee
(p. 158)

Carolina Chickadee
(p. 156)

black forehead

gray crest and upperparts

buffy flanks

Nesting: in a natural cavity or woodpecker cavity lined with soft vegetation, moss and animal hair; heavily spotted, white eggs are 1 x ½ in; female incubates 5–6 eggs for 12–14 days.

Did You Know?

Nesting pairs search for soft nest-lining material in late winter and may accept an offering of the hair that has accumulated in your hairbrush.

Look For

Easily identified by its gray crest and upperparts and black forehead, the Tufted Titmouse can often be seen at feeders.

White-breasted Nuthatch
Sitta carolinensis

Its upside-down antics and noisy, nasal call make the White-breasted Nuthatch a favorite among novice birders. Whether you spot this black-capped bullet spiraling headfirst down a tree or clinging to the underside of a branch in search of invertebrates, the nuthatch's odd behavior deserves a second glance. • The White-breasted Nuthatch is a common visitor to most backyard feeders, but it sticks around just long enough to grab a seed. Only an offering of suet can persuade this bird to remain in the same spot for any length of time.

Other ID: white underparts; white face; straight bill; short legs. *Female:* dark gray cap.
Size: L 5½–6 in; W 11 in.
Voice: song is a fast, nasal *yank-hank yank-hank*, lower than the Red-breasted Nuthatch; calls include *ha-ha-ha ha-ha-ha, ank ank* and *ip.*
Status: fairly common permanent resident with limited migratory wandering.
Habitat: mixed forests, woodlots and backyards.

Similar Birds

Red-breasted
Nuthatch

Carolina Chickadee
(p. 156)

Black-capped Chickadee
(p. 158)

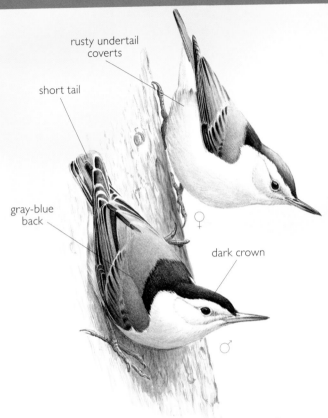

rusty undertail coverts

short tail

gray-blue back

dark crown

♀

♂

Nesting: in a natural cavity or an abandoned woodpecker nest; female lines the cavity with soft material; white eggs, speckled with brown, are ¾ x ⁹⁄₁₆ in; female incubates 5–8 eggs for 12–14 days.

Did You Know?

Nuthatches are presumably named for their habit of wedging seeds and nuts into crevices and hacking them open with their bills.

Look For

Nuthatches grasp the tree through foot power alone, unlike woodpeckers, which use their tails to brace themselves against tree trunks.

Carolina Wren
Thryothorus ludovicianus

The energetic, cheerful Carolina Wren can be shy and retiring, often hiding deep inside dense shrubbery. The best opportunity to view this vocal wren is when it sits on a conspicuous perch while unleashing its impressive song. Pairs perform lively duets at any time of day and in any season. The duet often begins with introductory chatter by the female, followed by innumerable ringing variations of *tea-kettle tea-kettle tea-kettle tea* from her mate. • Carolina Wrens readily nest in brushy, overgrown backyard thickets, or in obscure nooks or crevices in a house or barn. If conditions are favorable, two broods may be raised in a single season.

Other ID: rusty cheek; white throat; rather long tail for a wren.
Size: *L* 5½ in; *W* 7½ in.
Voice: loud, repetitious *tea-kettle tea-kettle tea-kettle;* female often chatters while male sings.
Status: common permanent resident in the south; uncommon to fairly common in the north.
Habitat: dense forest undergrowth, especially shrubby tangles and thickets.

Similar Birds

House Wren
(p. 166)

Winter Wren

Red-breasted
Nuthatch

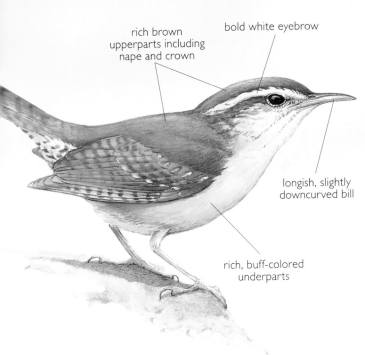

rich brown
upperparts including
nape and crown

bold white eyebrow

longish, slightly
downcurved bill

rich, buff-colored
underparts

Nesting: in a nest box or natural or artificial
cavity; nest is lined with soft materials, including
snakeskin at the entrance; brown-blotched, white
eggs are ¾ x ⁹⁄₁₆ in; female incubates 4–5 eggs
for 12–16 days.

Did You Know?

These wrens usually feed
near the ground on
insects and spiders but
can sometimes be seen
climbing tree trunks like
nuthatches.

Look For

Carolina Wrens sometimes
nest in hanging flowerpots on
porches or in cans or buckets
in open sheds and garages.

House Wren
Troglodytes aedon

With its bland, nondescript plumage, this suburban and woodland dweller can easily be overlooked, until you hear it sing a seemingly unending song in one breath. The voice of the House Wren is as sweet as that of a nightingale. • Despite its bubbly warble, this wren can be very aggressive toward other species that nest in its territory, puncturing and tossing eggs from other birds' nests. A House Wren often builds numerous nests, which later serve as decoys or "dummy" nests to fool would-be enemies.

Other ID: whitish throat; brown upperparts; whitish to buff underparts; faintly barred flanks.
Size: L 4½–5 in; W 6 in.
Voice: smooth, running, bubbly warble: *tsi-tsi-tsi-tsi oodle-oodle-oodle-oodle.*
Status: fairly common to common breeder; uncommon migrant; very rare winter visitor in southern New Jersey.
Habitat: thickets and shrubby openings in or at the edge of deciduous or mixed woodlands and residential areas; often in shrubs and thickets near buildings.

Similar Birds

Carolina Wren
(p. 164)

Winter Wren

short, upraised tail is finely barred with black

fine, dark barring on upper wings and lower back

faint buff eyebrow and eye ring

Nesting: in a natural or artificial cavity or abandoned woodpecker nest; nest of sticks and grass is lined with feathers and fur; heavily marked, white eggs are ⅝ x ½ in; female incubates 6–8 eggs for 12–15 days.

Did You Know?

This bird has the largest range of any New World passerine, stretching from Canada to southern South America.

Look For

Like all wrens, the House Wren usually holds its short tail upraised.

Eastern Bluebird
Sialia sialis

The Eastern Bluebird's enticing colors are like those of a warm setting sun against a deep blue sky. • This cavity nester's survival has been put to the test—populations declined in the presence of the competitive, introduced House Sparrow and European Starling. The removal of standing dead trees has also diminished nest site availability. Thankfully, bluebird enthusiasts and organizations have developed "bluebird trails"—mounted nest boxes on fence posts along highways, rural roads, and field edges—allowing Eastern Bluebird numbers to recover.

Other ID: dark bill; dark legs. *Female:* thin, white eye ring; gray-brown head and back are tinged with blue; blue wings and tail; paler chestnut underparts.
Size: L 7 in; W 13 in.
Voice: song is a rich, warbling *turr, turr-lee, turr-lee;* call is a chittering *pew.*
Status: fairly common breeder and migrant; uncommon in winter.
Habitat: cropland and pasture fencelines, meadows, fallow and abandoned fields, forest clearings and edges, golf courses, large lawns and cemeteries.

Similar Birds

Indigo Bunting
(p. 212)

Look For

The Eastern Bluebird uses an elevated perch as a base from which to hunt insects. It also feeds on berries and is especially attracted to wild grapes, sumac and currants.

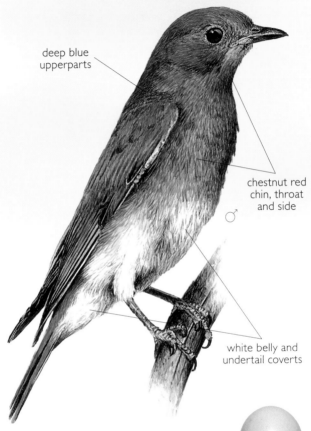

deep blue
upperparts

chestnut red
chin, throat
and side

♂

white belly and
undertail coverts

Nesting: in a natural cavity or nest box; female
builds a cup nest of grass, weed stems and small
twigs; pale blue eggs are ⅞ x ⅝ in; female incubates 4–5 eggs for 13–16 days.

Did You Know?

There are visible differences in the plumage of juvenile male
and female bluebirds. Both sexes are gray-brown with pale
streaking above and dark spotting below but males have
blue-tinged wings and tail.

Hermit Thrush
Catharus guttatus

True to its English name, the Hermit Thrush is always found alone. It migrates later in fall and earlier in spring than do the other spotted thrushes. • This bird is considered to be one of the finest singers of all of North America's birds. Similar to the song of the Swainson's Thrush, the song of the Hermit Thrush is almost always preceded with a single questioning note. • This thrush breeds locally in the highlands of northwestern New Jersey, as well as locally in the Pine Barrens.

Other ID: brown upperparts including head; underparts white with buffy flanks; often flicks its wings and slowly cocks its tail.
Size: *L* 7 in; *W* 11½ in.
Voice: song is a series of beautiful flutelike notes, both rising and falling in pitch; call is a dry *chuck*.
Status: fairly common migrant; uncommon and local breeder; uncommon winter visitor.
Habitat: most brushy or wooded habitats with leaf litter, especially near water.

Similar Birds

Swainson's Thrush   Veery   Fox Sparrow

pale eye ring

rusty wings

rusty tail

white throat
and breast with
black spotting

Nesting: in a small tree or shrub (occasionally on the ground); cup nest is built with grass, twigs and mud; light blue eggs are ⅞ x ⅝ in; female incubates 4 eggs for up to 13 days.

Did You Know?

This thrush feeds mainly on insects, worms and snails during the summer but adds a wide variety of fruit to its winter diet.

Look For

When alarmed, the Hermit Thrush flicks its wings, raises its tail and utters harsh *chuck* notes.

Wood Thrush
Hylocichla mustelina

The loud, warbled notes of the Wood Thrush once resounded through our woodlands, but forest fragmentation, increased nest parasitism by Brown-headed Cowbirds and urban sprawl have resulted in substantial population declines. Broken forests and diminutive woodlots have also allowed for the invasion of common, open-area predators, such as raccoons, skunks, crows and jays. Traditionally, these predators had little access to nests that were hidden deep within vast hardwood forests. Many disturbed forests now host families of American Robins rather than the once-prominent Wood Thrushes.

Other ID: plump body; streaked cheeks; brown wings, rump and tail.
Size: L 8 in; W 13 in.
Voice: *Male:* bell-like phrases of 3–5 notes, with each note at a different pitch and followed by a trill: *Will you live with me? Way up high in a tree, I'll come right down and…seeee!;* calls include a *pit pit* and *bweebeebeep*.
Status: uncommon breeder; scarce migrant; still fairly common locally in summer.
Habitat: moist, mature and preferably undisturbed deciduous woodlands and mixed forests.

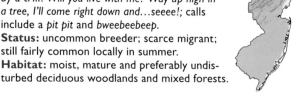

Similar Birds

American Robin
(p. 174)

Swainson's Thrush

Veery

bold, white eye ring

rusty head and back

large, black spots on white breast, sides and flanks

Nesting: low in a fork of a deciduous tree; female builds a bulky cup nest of vegetation, held together with mud and lined with softer materials; eggs are 1 x ¾ in; female incubates 3–4 pale, greenish blue eggs for 13–14 days.

Did You Know?

Henry David Thoreau considered the Wood Thrush's song to be the most beautiful of avian sounds. The male can even sing two notes at once!

Look For

Wood Thrushes forage on the ground or glean vegetation for insects and other invertebrates.

American Robin
Turdus migratorius

Come March, the familiar song of the American Robin may wake you early if you are a light sleeper. This abundant bird adapts easily to suburban areas and often works from dawn until after dusk when there is a nest to be built or hungry, young mouths to feed. • The robin's bright red belly contrasts with its dark head and wings, making this bird easy to identify. • In winter, fruit trees may attract flocks of robins, which gather to drink the fermenting fruit's intoxicating juices.

Other ID: incomplete, white eye ring; gray-brown back; white undertail coverts. *Juvenile:* spotted below; may be confused with spotted thrushes (e.g., Wood Thrush).
Size: *L* 10 in; *W* 17 in.
Voice: song is an evenly spaced warble: *cheerily cheer-up cheerio;* call is a rapid *tut-tut-tut.*
Status: common and widespread permanent resident; numbers are augmented in fall and winter, when large flocks may form.
Habitat: *Breeding:* residential lawns and gardens, pastures, urban parks, broken forests, bogs and river shorelines. *Winter:* near fruit-bearing trees and bushes.

Similar Birds

Wood Thrush
(p. 172)

Look For

A hunting robin with its head tilted to the side isn't listening for prey—it is actually looking for movements in the soil.

black head

dark gray head

black-tipped, yellow bill

white throat is streaked with black

♂ ♀

brick red breast is darker on male

Nesting: in a tree or shrub; cup nest is built of grass, moss, bark and mud; light blue eggs are 1⅛ x ¾ in; female incubates 4 eggs for 11–16 days; 2–3 broods per year.

Did You Know?

American Robins do not use nest boxes; they prefer platforms for their nests. Robins usually raise two broods per year, and the male cares for the fledglings from the first brood while the female incubates the second clutch of eggs.

Gray Catbird

Dumetella carolinensis

The Gray Catbird is an accomplished mimic that may fool you as it shuffles through under-brush and dense riparian shrubs, calling its catlike meow. Its mimicking talents are further enhanced by its ability to sing two notes at once, using each side of its syrinx individually. • The Gray Catbird is less prone to parasitism by Brown-headed Cowbirds because the female catbird is very loyal to her nest and is one of only a few species able to recognize and remove foreign eggs.

Other ID: dark gray overall; dark eyes, bill and legs.
Size: L 8½–9 in; W 11 in.
Voice: calls include a catlike *meoww* and a harsh *check-check;* song is a variety of warbles, squeaks and mimicked phrases interspersed with a *mew* call.
Status: fairly common breeder and migrant; scarce in mid-winter.
Habitat: dense thickets, brambles, shrubby or brushy areas, hedgerows and backyards, often near water.

Similar Birds

Northern Mockingbird
(p. 178)

Brown Thrasher
(p. 180)

black cap

long, dark gray
to black tail

rusty undertail
coverts

Nesting: in a dense shrub or thicket; bulky cup nest is made of twigs, leaves and grass; greenish blue eggs are ⅞ x ⅝ in; female incubates 4 eggs for 12–15 days.

Did You Know?

Dumetella, Latin for "small thicket," reflects the Gray Catbird's favorite habitat.

Look For

If you catch a glimpse of this bird during the breeding season, watch the male raise his long slender tail to show off his rust-colored undertail coverts.

Northern Mockingbird

Mimus polyglottos

The Northern Mockingbird has an amazing vocal repertoire that includes over 400 different song types, which it belts out incessantly throughout the breeding season, serenading into the night during a full moon. Mockingbirds can imitate almost anything. In some instances, they replicate notes so accurately that even computerized sound analysis is unable to detect the difference between the original source and the mockingbird's imitation.

Other ID: gray upperparts; 2 thin, white wing bars. *Juvenile:* paler overall; spotted breast.
Size: *L* 10 in; *W* 14 in.
Voice: song is a medley of mimicked phrases, with the phrases often repeated 3 or more times; calls include a harsh *chair* and *chewk*.
Status: common permanent resident in the south; uncommon to fairly common in the north; some populations have limited migratory movements.
Habitat: hedges, suburban gardens and orchard margins with an abundance of fruit; hedgerows of multiflora roses, especially in winter.

Similar Birds

Gray Catbird
(p. 176)

Brown Thrasher
(p. 180)

long, dark tail with white outer tail feathers

dark wings

thin, dark eye line

light underparts

Nesting: often in a small shrub or small tree; cup nest is built with twigs and plants; brown-blotched, bluish gray to greenish eggs are 1 x ⅝ in; female incubates 3–4 eggs for 12–13 days.

Did You Know?

The scientific name *polyglottos* is Greek for "many tongues" and refers to this bird's ability to mimic a wide variety of sounds.

Look For

The Northern Mockingbird's energetic territorial dance is delightful to watch, as males square off in what appears to be a swordless fencing duel.

Brown Thrasher
Toxostoma rufum

The Brown Thrasher has the streaked breast of a thrush and the long tail of a catbird, but it has a temper all its own. Because it nests close to the ground, the Brown Thrasher defends its nest with a vengeance, attacking snakes and other nest robbers sometimes to the point of drawing blood. • Biologists have estimated that the male Brown Thrasher is capable of producing up to 3000 distinctive song phrases—the most extensive vocal repertoire of any North American bird.

Other ID: reddish brown upperparts; long rufous tail; orange-yellow eyes.

Size: *L* 11½ in; *W* 13 in.

Voice: sings a large variety of phrases, with each phrase usually repeated twice: *dig-it dig-it, hoe-it hoe-it, pull-it-up pull-it-up;* calls include a loud crackling note, a harsh *shuck,* a soft *churr* or a whistled, 3-note *pit-cher-ee.*

Status: uncommon and declining permanent resident; numbers are augmented in migration and winter.

Habitat: dense shrubs and thickets, overgrown pastures, woodland edges and brushy areas, rarely close to urban areas.

Similar Birds

Wood Thrush
(p. 172)

Gray Catbird
(p. 176)

Northern Mockingbird
(p. 178)

gray cheek

long bill

2 white
wing bars

pale underparts with
heavy brown streaking

Nesting: usually in a low shrub; often on the
ground; cup nest is made of grass, twigs and
leaves, lined with vegetation; pale blue eggs dot-
ted with reddish brown are 1 x ¾ in; pair incubates 4 eggs for 11–14 days.

Did You Know?

Fencing off shrubby,
wooded areas bordering
wetlands and streams can
prevent cattle from devas-
tating thrasher nesting
habitat.

Look For

You might catch only a flash
of rufous as the Brown
Thrasher flies from one
thicket to another in its
shrubby understory habitat.

European Starling
Sturnus vulgaris

The European Starling did not hesitate to make itself known across North America after being released in New York's Central Park in 1890 and 1891. This highly adaptable bird not only took over the nest sites of native cavity nesters, such as Purple Martins, Tree Swallows and Red-headed Woodpeckers, but it also learned to mimic the sounds of Killdeer, Red-tailed Hawks, Soras and meadowlarks. • Look for European Starlings in massive evening roosts under bridges or on buildings in late summer and through the winter months.

Other ID: dark eyes; short, squared tail. *Nonbreeding:* feather tips are heavily spotted with white and buff; dark bill.
Size: *L* 8½ in; *W* 16 in.
Voice: variety of whistles, squeaks and gurgles; imitates other birds.
Status: very common permanent resident; numbers are augmented in fall and winter; some populations have migratory movements.
Habitat: cities, towns, residential areas, feedlots, farmyards and clearings.

Similar Birds

Brown-headed Cowbird
(p. 220)

Common Grackle
(p. 218)

iridescent, purple-black head, neck and breast

glossy, green back with buffy spots

yellow bill

greenish black underparts

breeding

Nesting: in an abandoned woodpecker cavity, natural cavity or nest box; nest is made of grass, twigs and straw; bluish to greenish white eggs are 1⅛ x ⅞ in; female incubates 4–6 eggs for 12–14 days.

Did You Know?

Starlings were brought to New York as part of the Shakespeare society's plan to introduce all the birds mentioned in their favorite author's writings.

Look For

This bird can be confused with a blackbird, but note the European Starling's shorter tail and longer bill.

Cedar Waxwing
Bombycilla cedrorum

With its black mask and slick hairdo, the Cedar Waxwing has a heroic look. This bird's splendid personality is reflected in its amusing antics after it gorges on fermented berries and in its gentle courtship dance. To court a mate, the gentlemanly male hops toward a female and offers her a berry. The female accepts the berry and hops away, then stops and hops back toward the male to offer him the berry in return. • If a bird's crop is full and it is unable to eat any more, it will continue to pluck fruit and pass it down the line, like a bucket brigade, until the fruit is gulped down by a still-hungry bird.

Other ID: brown upperparts; gray rump; white undertail coverts. *Juvenile:* blurry, dark streaks below.
Size: *L* 7 in; *W* 12 in.
Voice: faint, high-pitched, trilled whistle: *tseee-tseee-tseee.*
Status: uncommon to fairly common breeder; fairly common in fall; uncommon in winter, but may be seen in medium-sized flocks.
Habitat: wooded residential parks and gardens, overgrown fields, forest edges and second-growth, riparian or open woodlands; often near fruit trees and water.

Similar Birds

Bohemian Waxwing

Look For

Waxwings, like starlings, are almost always found in flocks during the nonbreeding season, which can confuse novice birdwatchers.

cinnamon crest

black mask

small red "drops" on wings

yellow wash on belly

yellow terminal tail band

Nesting: in a tree or shrub; cup nest is made of twigs, moss and lichen; darkly spotted, bluish to gray eggs are ⅞ x ⅝ in; female incubates 3–5 eggs for 12–16 days.

Did You Know?

The Bohemian Waxwing (*B. garrulus*) is an extremely rare winter visitor and is only seen casually in New Jersey. It is slightly larger than the Cedar Waxwing and has rufous undertail coverts and more rufous in its face.

Yellow Warbler

Dendroica petechia

The Yellow Warbler's nest is often parasitized by the Brown-headed Cowbird, but the warbler can recognize cowbird eggs, and rather than tossing them out, it will build another nest overtop the old eggs or abandon the nest completely. Occasionally, cowbirds strike repeatedly—a five-story nest was once found! • The widely distributed Yellow Warbler arrives in May, flitting from branch to branch in search of juicy caterpillars, aphids and beetles and singing its *sweet-sweet* song. It—and the American Goldfinch—are often mistakenly called "Wild Canary."

Other ID: bright yellow body; pale legs; black bill. *Female:* may have faint, red breast streaks.
Size: L 5 in; W 8 in.
Voice: song is a fast, frequently repeated *sweet-sweet-sweet summer sweet*.
Status: fairly common breeder and migrant.
Habitat: dense, moist scrub, scrubby meadows and marshes, second-growth edge, riparian woodland, parks and gardens.

Similar Birds

American Goldfinch
(p. 226)

Common Yellowthroat
(p. 194)

Wilson's Warbler

beady,
dark eyes

♀

♂

olive wings and
tail with bright
yellow barring

red breast streaks

Nesting: in a deciduous tree or shrub; female
builds a cup nest of grass, weeds and shredded
bark; darkly speckled, greenish white eggs are
⅝ x ½ in; female incubates eggs for 11–12 days.

Did You Know?

The Yellow Warbler has
an amazing geographical
range. It is found throughout North America and
on islands in Central
and South America.

Look For

In fall, when male Yellow
Warblers are no longer in
breeding plumage, look for
flashes of yellow on the sides
of their tails to identify them.

Yellow-rumped Warbler

Dendroica coronata

Yellow-rumped Warblers are the most abundant and widespread wood-warblers in North America. Bayberry, juniper and sumac trees laden with berries attract these birds in winter. • This species comes in two forms: the common, white-throated "Myrtle Warbler" of the East, and the yellow-throated "Audubon's Warbler" of the West, which is a casual vagrant in New Jersey. Although Myrtles rarely breed in New Jersey, they are common during migration, as well as in the south and along the coast in winter.

Other ID: 2 white wing bars; heavily streaked underparts; bright yellow rump. *Breeding male:* black cheek and breast band. *Breeding female:* gray-brown upperparts.
Size: L 5½ in; W 9¼ in.
Voice: song is a brief, bubbling warble rising or falling at the end; call is a sharp *chip* or *chet*.
Status: common migrant and winter visitor; during winter, most numerous along the coast and in southern New Jersey.
Habitat: well-vegetated, lowland habitats; prefers wax myrtle thickets in late fall and winter.

Similar Birds

Black-throated Green Warbler

Cape May Warbler

Magnolia Warbler

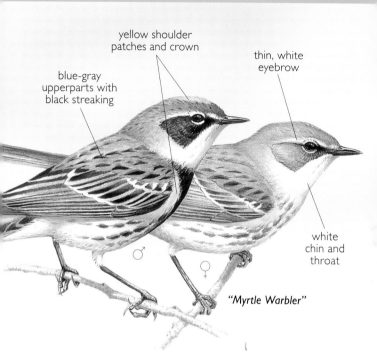

blue-gray uppparts with black streaking

yellow shoulder patches and crown

thin, white eyebrow

white chin and throat

♂

♀

"Myrtle Warbler"

Nesting: rarely nests in New Jersey; in a crotch or on a horizontal limb in a conifer; cup nest is made of vegetation and spider silk; brown-blotched, buff-colored eggs are ⅝ x ½ in; female incubates 4–5 eggs for up to 13 days.

Did You Know?

This small warbler's habit of flitting near buildings to snatch spiders from their webs has earned it the nickname "Spider Bird."

Look For

Small puddles that form during or after rains often attract warblers, allowing a glimpse of these secretive birds.

Black-and-white Warbler

Mniotilta varia

Striped plumage and their unusual foraging behavior of creeping along the trunks and larger branches of trees distinguish Black-and-white Warblers from most of their kin. Though they will join other warblers at gleaning insects and spiders from the outer branches, their preference for feeding on the trunk and inner branches helps these specialized warblers avoid competition with close family members. • This warbler is one of the first arrivals on spring breeding grounds, appearing in New Jersey by mid-April.

Other ID: *Breeding male:* black cheek patch and throat separated by white "mustache"; white underparts heavily streaked with black. *Nonbreeding male:* white throat. *Female:* white cheek and throat; underparts less boldly streaked and washed with pale buff on flanks.
Size: 5¼ in; W 8¼ in.
Voice: call is a soft, high *seet*; song is a series of high, thin 2-syllable notes.
Status: fairly common breeder and migrant.
Habitat: any wooded habitat.

Similar Birds

Yellow-throated Warbler

Blackpoll Warbler

upperparts mostly black
with white streaks

white
eyebrow

black crown
with white
median stripe

♂

♀

black wings
with 2 white
wing bars

breeding

Nesting: usually on the ground, in a sheltered hollow; cup nest of vegetation is lined with fur and fine grasses; darkly flecked, creamy white eggs are ⅝ x ½ in; female incubates 4–5 eggs for 11 days.

Did You Know?

This bird's scientific name *varia* means "varied," in reference to its plumage.

Look For

These birds share their tree-creeping behavior with nuthatches, creepers and Yellow-throated Warblers, which look similar if their yellow throat is hidden.

American Redstart
Setophaga ruticilla

The American Redstart is a favorite among birders. Few birds can rival a mature male redstart for his contrasting black and orange plumage, approach-ability and animated behavior. • In its pursuit of prey, the American Redstart flushes insects with a flash of color from its wings or tail. It then uses its broad bill and rictal bristles (the short, whiskerlike feathers around its mouth) to capture insects, like an expert flycatcher. • On its wintering grounds, the American Redstart is known as "Butterfly Bird," and in Latin America it is known as Candelita or "little torch."

Other ID: *Male:* white belly and undertail coverts. *Female:* white underparts. *Immature male:* resembles female but with orange shoulder patches and dark face.

Size: *L* 5 in; *W* 8½ in.

Voice: male's song is a highly variable series of *tseet* or *zee* notes at different pitches; call is a sharp, sweet *chip*.

Status: fairly common breeder and migrant.

Habitat: shrubby woodland edges; open and semi-open forest with a regenerating deciduous understory. *In migration:* prefers woodland edge and thickets.

Look For

The American Redstart is always in motion. Even when perched, this bird continues to flicker and often spreads its feathers and fans its tail, showing off the colorful patches at the base of its outer tail feathers.

yellow foreshoulder, wing and tail patches

olive brown upperparts

black head and upperparts

♀

♂

reddish orange foreshoulder, wing and tail patches

Nesting: in a shrub or sapling; female builds an open cup nest of plant down, bark shreds, grass and rootlets; brown-marked, whitish eggs are ⅝ x ½ in; female incubates 4 eggs for 11–12 days.

Did You Know?

This bird's high-pitched, lisping songs are so variable that identifying an American Redstart by song alone is a challenge for birders of all levels. Even experienced birders who are faced with an unknown warbler song will exclaim, "It must be a redstart!"

Common Yellowthroat

Geothlypis trichas

The bumblebee colors of the male Common Yellowthroat's black mask and yellow throat identify this skulking wetland resident. He sings his *witchety* song from strategically chosen cattail perches that he visits in rotation, fiercely guarding his territory against the intrusion of other males. • The Common Yellowthroat is different from most wood-warblers, preferring marshlands and wet, overgrown meadows to forests. The female has no mask and remains mostly hidden from view in thick vegetation when she tends to the nest.

Other ID: black bill; fleshy legs. *Female:* yellow throat and upper breast; yellow undertail coverts; whitish vent.
Size: *L* 5 in; *W* 7 in.
Voice: song is a clear, oscillating *witchety witchety witchety-witch*; call is a sharp, buzzy *tcheck* or *tchet*.
Status: fairly common breeder and migrant.
Habitat: cattail marshes, sedge wetlands, riparian areas, beaver ponds and wet, overgrown meadows; sometimes dry field edges.

Similar Birds

Kentucky Warbler

Wilson's Warbler

olive green to olive brown upperparts

♀

dingy white belly

broad, black mask with white upper border

yellow throat and breast

♂

Nesting: on or near the ground or in a small shrub or emergent vegetation; female builds an open cup nest of weeds, grass, bark strips and moss; brown-blotched, white eggs are ⅝ x ½ in; female incubates 3–5 eggs for 12 days.

Did You Know?

Swedish biologist Carolus Linnaeus named the Common Yellowthroat in 1766, making it one of the first North American birds to be described.

Look For

Common Yellowthroats immerse themselves or roll in water, then shake off the excess water by flicking or flapping their wings.

Scarlet Tanager
Piranga olivacea

The breeding male Scarlet Tanager's vibrant red plumage graces the canopies in wooded ravines and migrant stopover sites, so birders tend to hear this bird long before they see it. This much anticipated migrant announces its arrival with a whistled song, reminiscent of a slurred version of the American Robin's. • The Scarlet Tanager has the longest migration route of all tanager species and is one of two tanager species that routinely nest in New Jersey.

Other ID: *Female* and *nonbreeding male:* uniformly olive upperparts; yellow underparts; grayish wings, possibly tinged with brown; yellow eye ring.
Size: *L* 7 in; *W* 11½ in.
Voice: song is a series of 4–5 sweet, clear, whistled phrases; call is *chip-burrr* or *chip-churrr.*
Status: fairly common breeder and migrant.
Habitat: fairly mature, upland deciduous and mixed forests. *In migration:* coastal shrubbery.

Similar Birds

Summer Tanager

Northern Cardinal (p. 208)

Baltimore Oriole (p. 222)

Orchard Oriole

pale bill

bright red body

pure black wings
and tail

♀

♂

breeding

Nesting: high in a deciduous tree; female builds a flimsy, shallow cup nest of grass, weeds and twigs; brown-spotted, pale blue-green eggs are ⅞ x ⅝ in; female incubates 2–5 eggs for 12–14 days.

Did You Know?

In Central and South America, there are over 200 tanager species in every color imaginable.

Look For

Scarlet Tanagers forage in the forest understory in cold, rainy weather, making them easier to observe.

Eastern Towhee
Pipilo erythrophthalmus

Eastern Towhees are large, colorful members of the sparrow family. These noisy birds are often heard before they are seen as they rustle about in dense undergrowth, craftily scraping back layers of leaves to expose the seeds, berries or insects hidden beneath. They employ an unusual two-footed technique to uncover food items—a strategy that is especially important in winter when virtually all of their food is taken from the ground. • The Eastern Towhee and its western relative, the Spotted Towhee *(P. maculata)*, were once grouped together as the "Rufous-sided Towhee."

Other ID: white lower breast and belly; buff undertail coverts; eyes are commonly red. *In flight:* white outer tail corners.
Size: *L* 7–8½ in; *W* 10½ in.
Voice: song is 2 high whistled notes followed by a trill: *drink your teeeee;* call is a scratchy, slurred *cheweee!* or *chewink!*
Status: uncommon permanent resident and migrant; numbers have likely declined due to loss of habitat.
Habitat: along woodland edges, hedgerows and in shrubby, abandoned fields.

Look For

Showy towhees are sometimes attracted to feeders, where they scratch on the ground for millet, oats or sunflower seeds.

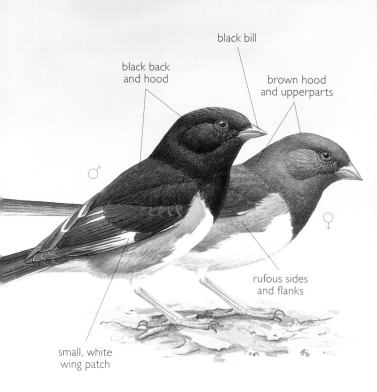

black back
and hood

black bill

brown hood
and upperparts

♂

♀

rufous sides
and flanks

small, white
wing patch

Nesting: on the ground or low in a dense shrub; female builds a cup nest of twigs, bark strips, grass and animal hair; pale, brown-spotted, creamy eggs are ⅞ x ⅝ in; mainly the female incubates 3–4 eggs for 12–13 days.

Did You Know?

The scientific name *Pipilo* is derived from the Latin *pipo*, meaning "to chirp or peep," and *erythrophthalmus* means "red eye" in Greek, though towhees in the southeastern states may have white or orange irises.

Chipping Sparrow
Spizella passerina

Though you may spot the relatively tame Chipping Sparrow singing from a high perch, it commonly nests at eye level, so you can easily watch its breeding and nest-building rituals. You can even take part in the building of this bird's nest by leaving samples of your pet's hair—or your own—around your backyard. • This bird's song is very similar to that of the Dark-eyed Junco. Listen for a slightly faster, drier and less musical series of notes to identify the Chipping Sparrow.

Other ID: *Breeding:* mottled brown upperparts; light gray, unstreaked underparts; dark bill. *Nonbreeding:* brownish crown with dark streaks; brown cheek; dark eye line and whisker; pale lower mandible.
Size: *L* 5–6 in; *W* 8½ in.
Voice: song is a rapid, dry trill of *chip* notes; call is a high-pitched *chip*.
Status: fairly common breeder and migrant; rare and only in the south in winter.
Habitat: open conifers or mixed woodland edges; farms; yards and gardens with tree and shrub borders.

Similar Birds

American Tree Sparrow   Field Sparrow   Swamp Sparrow

prominent rufous cap

white eyebrow

black eye line

white wing bars

breeding

Nesting: usually at mid-level in a coniferous tree; female builds a cup nest of grass and rootlets lined with hair; pale blue eggs are ¾ x ½ in; female incubates 4 eggs for 11–12 days.

Did You Know?

The Chipping Sparrow is the most common and widely distributed migrating sparrow in North America.

Look For

Chipping Sparrows forage on lawns and in weedy fields for the seeds of grasses, dandelions and clovers; they occasionally visit feeders.

Song Sparrow
Melospiza melodia

The well-named Song Sparrow is among the great singers of the bird world. By the time a young male Song Sparrow is a few months old, he has already created a courtship tune of his own, having learned the basics of melody and rhythm by overhearing his father and rival males. • In winter, adaptable Song Sparrows are common throughout much of New Jersey and inhabit woodland edges, weedy ditches, field edges and riparian thickets. They regularly visit backyard feeders, belting out their sweet, three-part song throughout the year.

Other ID: white jaw line with dark mustache; mottled brown upperparts; rounded tail tip.
Size: *L* 6–7 in; *W* 8 in.
Voice: song is 1–4 introductory notes, such as *sweet sweet sweet,* followed by a buzzy *towee,* then a short, descending trill; call is a short *tsip* or *tchep.*
Status: fairly common breeder; common in migration and winter.
Habitat: shrubs, riparian thickets, forest openings and pastures, often near water; parks and gardens.

Similar Birds

Swamp Sparrow

Fox Sparrow

Savannah Sparrow

brown line
behind eye

dark crown with
pale central stripe

grayish face

heavy brown streaks
converge at central
breast spot

Nesting: usually on the ground or in a low
shrub; female builds an open cup nest of grass,
weeds and bark strips; brown-blotched, greenish white eggs are ⅞ x ⅝ in; female incubates
3–5 eggs for 12–14 days.

Did You Know?

Though female songbirds
are not usually vocal, the
female Song Sparrow will
occasionally sing a tune of
her own.

Look For

The Song Sparrow pumps its
long, rounded tail in flight. It
also often issues a high-
pitched *seet* flight call.

White-throated Sparrow

Zonotrichia albicollis

During migration and winter, White-throated Sparrows forage mostly on the ground. They kick aside the leaf litter and eat seeds and insects that they find underneath. Their bold, white throat and striped crown can be confused only with the White-crowned Sparrow *(Z. leucophrys);* both species are found in open, bushy habitats and farmlands, but White-throats also frequent forested woodlands. • Two color morphs are common: one has black and white stripes on the head; the other has brown and tan stripes.

Other ID: gray cheek; black eye line; unstreaked, gray underparts; mottled brown upperparts.
Size: *L* 6½–7½ in; *W* 9 in.
Voice: variable song is a clear, distinct, whistled: *Old Sam Peabody, Peabody, Peabody;* call is a sharp *chink.*
Status: common migrant and winter visitor; very rare breeder in the northwest highlands.
Habitat: woodlots, wooded parks and riparian brush.

Similar Birds

White-crowned
Sparrow

Look For

This sparrow cleans and sharpens its bill by wiping it on a hard surface.

black-and-white
(or brown-and-tan)
striped head

yellow
lores

grayish
bill

white
throat

Nesting: nests very rarely in New Jersey; on or near the ground, often concealed by a low shrub or fallen log; open cup nest of grass plant material is lined with fine grass and hair; bluish, spotted eggs are 7/8 x 9/16 in; female incubates 4–5 eggs for 11–14 days.

Did You Know?

During migration, White-throated Sparrows are often found in large, loose, active bands with other sparrows, sometimes acting like sentinels on the look-out for neighborhood cats and other predators.

Dark-eyed Junco

Junco hyemalis

Juncos usually congregate in backyards with bird feeders and sheltering conifers. They rarely perch at feeders, preferring to snatch up seeds that are knocked to the ground by other visitors, such as chickadees, nuthatches and other sparrows. • This bird will flash its distinctive white outer tail feathers as it rushes for cover after being flushed. • Look for juncos in the highland of northwestern New Jersey in summer and at backyard feeders and brushy woodlands statewide in winter.

Other ID: *Female:* gray-brown where the male is slate gray.
Size: L 6–7 in; W 9 in.
Voice: song is a long, dry trill; call is a smacking *chip* note, often given in series.
Status: common late-fall migrant and winter visitor; uncommon in spring; scarce and local breeder.
Habitat: shrubby woodland borders, weedy yards and backyard feeders.

Look For

Dark-eyed Juncos spend most of their time on the ground and can often be seen foraging on lawns. They usually hop forward but will also hop sideways when chasing insects.

pale pink bill

dark slate gray overall

white outer tail feathers

♂

white belly and undertail coverts

"Slate-colored Junco"

Nesting: rarely nests in New Jersey; on the ground, usually concealed; female builds a cup nest of twigs, grass, bark and moss; brown-marked, whitish to bluish eggs are ¾ x ½ in; female incubates 3–5 eggs for 12–13 days.

Did You Know?

There are five closely related Dark-eyed Junco subspecies in North America that share similar habits but differ in coloration and breeding range. Dark-eyed Juncos seen in New Jersey belong to the subspecies *hyemalis,* also known as the "Slate-colored Junco."

Northern Cardinal
Cardinalis cardinalis

A male Northern Cardinal displays his vibrant red crest and raises his tail when he is excited or agitated. He vigorously defends his territory, even attacking his own reflection in a window or hubcap. • Cardinals are some of only a few bird species to maintain strong pair bonds. Some couples sing to each other year-round, while others join loose flocks, re-establishing pair bonds in spring during a "courtship feeding." During this ritual, the male offers a seed to the female, which she then accepts and eats.

Other ID: *Male:* red overall. *Female:* brownish buff overall; fainter mask; orangy crest, wings and tail.
Size: *L* 8–9 in; *W* 12 in.
Voice: call is a metallic *chip;* song is series of clear, bubbly whistled notes: *What cheer! What cheer! birdie-birdie-birdie what cheer!*
Status: common permanent resident; some populations have very limited migratory movements, if any.
Habitat: brushy thickets and shrubby tangles along forest and woodland edges; backyards and urban and suburban parks.

Similar Birds

Summer Tanager

Scarlet Tanager
(p. 196)

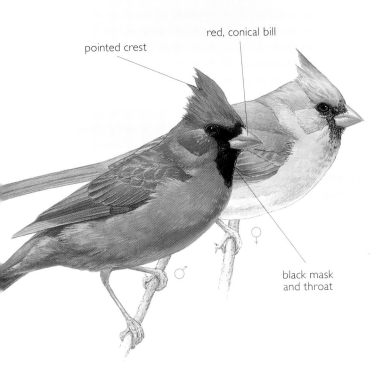

pointed crest

red, conical bill

black mask
and throat

♂ ♀

Nesting: in a dense shrub, vine tangle, or low
in a coniferous tree; female builds an open cup
nest of twigs, grass and shredded bark; brown-
blotched, white to greenish white eggs are
1 x ¾ in; female incubates 3–4 eggs for
12–13 days.

Did You Know?

This bird owes its name
to the vivid red plumage
of the male, which resem-
bles the robes of Roman
Catholic cardinals.

Look For

A cardinal uses its bill to peel
the skin off a grape before
eating the pulp and the seed.

Rose-breasted Grosbeak

Pheucticus ludovicianus

Whistling its unhurried tune, the Rose-breasted Grosbeak sounds like a robin that has taken singing lessons. Although the female lacks the magnificent colors of the male, she shares his talent for beautiful song. • Mating grosbeaks often touch bills during courtship and after absences. • These grosbeaks usually build their nests low in a tree or tall shrub. By contrast, they typically forage high in the canopy, where they can be difficult to spot. Luckily for birders, the abundance of berries in fall often draws these birds closer to ground level.

Other ID: dark tail. *Male:* red breast and inner underwings. *Female:* thin crown stripe; brown upperparts; buff underparts with dark brown streaking.
Size: L 7–8½ in; W 12½ in.
Voice: song is a long, melodious series of whistled notes, much like a fast version of a robin's song; call is a distinctive squeak.
Status: fairly common summer resident and migrant statewide.
Habitat: deciduous and mixed forests.

Similar Birds

Purple Finch, female

Look For

Grosbeaks have large, pale (dusky in fall) bills that distinguish them from sparrows and finches, which have smaller conical bills.

pale,
conical bill

black hood
and back

bold, whitish
eyebrow

♀

♂

dark wings with
small white
patches

white underparts
and rump

Nesting: fairly low in a tree or tall shrub, often near water; mostly the female builds a flimsy cup nest of plant material, lined with rootlets and hair; greenish blue, spotted eggs are 1 x ⅝ in; pair incubates 3–5 eggs for 13–14 days.

Did You Know?

The species name *ludovicianus*, Latin for "from Louisiana," is somewhat misleading because this bird is only a migrant through Louisiana and other southern states.

Indigo Bunting
Passerina cyanea

The vivid, electric blue adult male Indigo Bunting is one of the most spectacular birds in New Jersey. These birds arrive in April or May and favor woodland edges, thickets and power-line cuts. • The male is a persistent singer, vocalizing even through the heat of a summer day. A young male doesn't learn his couplet song from his parents but from neighboring males during his first year on his own. • Planting coneflowers, cosmos or foxtail grasses may attract Indigo Buntings to your backyard.

Other ID: beady black eyes; black legs; no wing bars. *Nonbreeding male:* similar to female, but with some blue in wings and tail. *Female:* soft, warm brown overall; whitish throat.
Size: *L* 5½ in; *W* 8 in.
Voice: song consists of paired warbled whistles: *fire-fire, where-where, here-here, see-it see-it;* call is a quick *spit*.
Status: fairly common breeder and migrant.
Habitat: deciduous forest and woodland edges, regenerating forest clearings, orchards and shrubby fields.

Similar Birds

Blue Grosbeak

Eastern Bluebird
(p. 168)

dark blue head

black lores

gray, conical bill

♂

♀

wings and tail
may show
some brown

faint brown
streaks on breast

breeding

Nesting: in a small tree, shrub or within a vine
tangle; female builds a cup nest of grass, leaves
and bark strips; unmarked, white to bluish white
eggs are ¾ x ½ in; female incubates 3–4 eggs
for 12–13 days.

Did You Know?

Females choose the most
melodious males as mates,
because these males can
usually establish territories
with the finest habitat.

Look For

The Indigo Bunting will land
midway on a stem of grass
and shuffle slowly toward the
seedhead, twitching its tail
and bending down the stem
to reach the seeds.

Red-winged Blackbird

Agelaius phoeniceus

The male Red-winged Blackbird wears his bright red shoulders like armor—together with his short, raspy song, they are key in defending his territory from rivals. In field experiments, males whose red shoulders were painted black soon lost their territories. • Nearly every cattail marsh worthy of note in New Jersey hosts Red-winged Blackbirds during at least part of the year. • The female's sparrow-like, cryptic coloration allows her to sit inconspicuously on her nest.

Other ID: *Male:* black overall. *Female:* mottled brown upperparts; pale eyebrow. *Immature male:* resembles female with suggestion of red in wing.
Size: *L* 7½–9 in; *W* 13 in.
Voice: song is a loud, raspy *konk-a-ree* or *ogle-reeeee;* calls include a harsh *check* and high *tse-ert;* female gives a loud *che-che-che chee chee chee.*
Status: common, widespread breeder and migrant; also common in winter but more localized, forming large flocks, often with other blackbirds.
Habitat: *Summer* and *in migration:* cattail marshes, wet meadows and ditches, croplands and shoreline shrubs. *Winter:* residential areas.

Similar Birds

Rusty Blackbird   Brown-headed Cowbird
                         (p. 220)

red shoulder
patch edged
in yellow

♂

pale pinkish
throat

heavily streaked
underparts

♀

Nesting: in cattails, shoreline bushes or wet meadows; female builds an open cup nest of dried cattail leaves lined with fine grass; darkly marked, pale bluish green eggs are 1 x ¾ in; female incubates 3–4 eggs for 10–12 days.

Did You Know?

Some scientists believe that the Red-winged Blackbird is the most abundant bird species in North America.

Look For

As he sings his *konk-a-ree* song, the male Red-winged Blackbird spreads his shoulders to display his bright red wing patch to rivals and potential mates.

Eastern Meadowlark
Sturnella magna

The drab dress of most female songbirds protects them during the breeding season, but the female Eastern Meadowlark uses a different strategy. Her V-shaped "necklace" and bright yellow throat and belly create a colorful distraction as she bursts from the grass to lead predators away from her nest. A flushed female will never abandon her chicks, but her extra vigilance following a threat can result in less frequent feedings for the nestlings. • Eastern Meadowlark numbers are declining in New Jersey, primarily due to habitat loss.

Other ID: mottled, rich brown upperparts; long, sharp bill; blackish crown stripes and eye line border pale eyebrow and median crown stripe; long, fleshy legs. *Nonbreeding:* duller plumage.
Size: *L* 9–9½ in; *W* 14 in.
Voice: song is a rich series of 2–8 melodic, clear, slurred whistles: *see-you at school-today* or *this is the year;* gives a rattling flight call and a buzzy *dzeart.*
Status: scarce, local and declining breeder; local and uncommon in migration and winter.
Habitat: grassy meadows, pastures and roadsides, marsh edges and croplands, coastal barrens in migration and winter.

Similar Birds

Dickcissel

Look For

The Eastern Meadowlark often sings from fence posts and power lines. Its song is the best way to tell the Eastern from the Western Meadowlark, which is rare in New Jersey.

white jaw line

yellow lores

dark streaking on buff flanks

short, wide tail with white outer tail feathers

broad, black breast band on yellow underparts

breeding

Nesting: in a concealed depression on the ground; female builds a domed grass nest, woven into surrounding vegetation; heavily spotted, white eggs are 1⅛ x ¾ in; female incubates 3–7 eggs for 13–15 days.

Did You Know?

This bird likely got its name because its song reminded early settlers of the song of the Skylark (*Alauda arvensis*) of Europe. But the Eastern Meadowlark is not a lark at all—it is actually a brightly colored member of the blackbird family. Its silhouette reveals its blackbird features.

Common Grackle
Quiscalus quiscula

The Common Grackle is a poor but spirited singer. Usually while perched in a shrub, a male grackle will slowly take a deep breath to inflate his breast, causing his feathers to spike outward, then close his eyes and give out a loud, strained *tssh-schleek*. Despite his lack of musical talent, the male remains smug and proud, posing with his bill held high.

Other ID: long, keeled tail. *Female:* smaller, duller and browner than male. *Juvenile:* dull brown overall; dark eyes.
Size: *L* 11–13½ in; *W* 17 in.
Voice: song is a series of harsh, strained notes ending with a metallic squeak: *tssh-schleek* or *gri-de-leeek;* call is a quick, loud *swaaaack* or *chaack*.
Status: common and widespread permanent resident, though individuals present in summer may be different from those in winter; joins large mixed flocks in the nonbreeding season.
Habitat: wetlands, hedgerows, fields and croplands; meadows and woodlands; shrubby urban and suburban areas.

Similar Birds

Rusty Blackbird

Boat-tailed Grackle

European Starling
(p. 182)

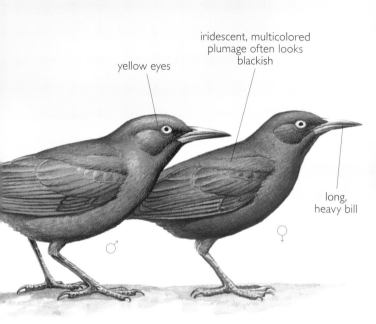

yellow eyes

iridescent, multicolored plumage often looks blackish

long, heavy bill

♂

♀

Nesting: singly or in small colonies; in dense trees (particularly planted conifers), shrubs or emergent vegetation; female builds a bulky, open cup nest of twigs, grass, plant fibers and mud and lines it with fine grass or feathers; brown-blotched, pale blue eggs are 1⅛ x ⅞ in; female incubates 4–5 eggs for 12–14 days.

Did You Know?

Grackles commonly flock with European Starlings, Red-winged Blackbirds and Brown-headed Cowbirds.

Look For

The Common Grackle has a long, heavy bill and lengthy, wedge-shaped tail that trails behind in flight and is most obvious in breeding males.

Brown-headed Cowbird

Molothrus ater

These nomads historically followed bison herds across the Great Plains (they now follow cattle), so they never stayed in one area long enough to build and tend a nest. Instead, cowbirds lay their eggs in other birds' nests, relying on the unsuspecting adoptive parents to incubate the eggs and feed the young. Orioles, warblers, vireos and tanagers are among the most affected species. Increased livestock farming and fragmentation of forests has encouraged the expansion of the cowbird's range. It is known to parasitize more than 140 bird species.

Other ID: thick, conical bill; short, squared tail.
Size: *L* 6–8 in; *W* 12 in.
Voice: song is a high, liquidy gurgle: *glug-ahl-whee* or *bubbloozeee;* call is a squeaky, high-pitched *seep, psee* or *wee-tse-tse* or fast, chipping *ch-ch-ch-ch-ch-ch.*
Status: fairly common to common permanent resident; numbers are augmented in migration and winter.
Habitat: areas near cattle or horses, woodland edges, utility rights-of-way, roadsides, landfills and backyard feeders.

Similar Birds

Rusty Blackbird

Red-winged Blackbird
(p. 214)

dark eyes

pale throat

dark brown head

light brown plumage

♀

♂

iridescent, green-blue plumage looks glossy black

Nesting: does not build a nest; female lays up to 40 eggs a year in the nests of other birds, usually 1 egg per nest; brown-speckled, whitish eggs are ⅞ x ⅝ in; eggs hatch after 10–13 days.

Did You Know?

When courting a female, the male cowbird points his bill upward, fans his tail and wings and utters a loud *squeek*.

Look For

When cowbirds feed in flocks, they hold their back ends up high, with their tails sticking straight up in the air.

Baltimore Oriole
Icterus galbula

With a flutelike song and a preference for the canopies of neighborhood trees, the Baltimore Oriole is difficult to spot. A hanging pouch nest dangling in a bare tree in fall and winter is sometimes the only evidence that the bird was there at all. The nests are deceptively strong and often remain intact through the harshest weather. • The male's plumage mirrors the colors of the coat of arms of Sir George Calvert, Baron of Baltimore, who established the first colony in Maryland.

Other ID: *Female* and *immature:* olive brown upperparts (darkest on head).
Size: *L* 7–8 in; *W* 11½ in.
Voice: song consists of slow, clear whistles: *peter peter peter here peter;* calls include a 2-note *tea-too* and a rapid chatter: *ch-ch-ch-ch.*
Status: fairly common breeder and migrant; very rare in winter, usually at feeders.
Habitat: deciduous and mixed forests, particularly riparian woodlands, natural openings and edges, orchards, gardens and parklands.

Similar Birds

Orchard Oriole

Scarlet Tanager
(p. 196)

thin, whitish
wing bars

black hood, back,
wings and central
tail feathers

thick, orange
wing bar

♀

♂

dull yellow-
orange under-
parts and rump

bright orange underparts,
shoulder, rump and outer
tail feathers

Nesting: high in a deciduous tree; female builds a hanging pouch nest of grass, shredded bark and grapevines; darkly marked, pale gray to bluish white eggs are ⅞ x ⅝ in; female incubates 4–5 eggs for 12–14 days.

Did You Know?

Orioles spend more than half of each year in the tropics of Central and South America.

Look For

You can sometimes see a Baltimore Oriole at a feeder, especially if orange halves are offered.

House Finch
Carpodacus mexicanus

A native to western North America, the House Finch was brought to eastern parts of the continent as an illegally captured cage bird known as the "Hollywood Finch." In the early 1940s, New York pet shop owners released their birds to avoid prosecution and fines, and it is likely the descendants of those birds that have colonized our area. In fact, the House Finch is now commonly found throughout the continental U.S. and has been introduced in Hawaii. • Only the resourceful House Finch has been aggressive and stubborn enough to successfully outcompete the House Sparrow. Both birds flourish in urban environments.

Other ID: streaked undertail coverts. *Female:* indistinct facial patterning; heavily streaked underparts.
Size: L 5–6 in; W 9½ in.
Voice: song is a bright, disjointed warble lasting about 3 seconds, often ending with a harsh *jeeer* or *wheer;* flight call is a sweet *cheer*, given singly or in series.
Status: common permanent resident; some limited migratory movement.
Habitat: cities, towns and agricultural areas.

Similar Birds

Purple Finch

Look For

In flight, the House Finch has a square tail, whereas the similar-looking Purple Finch has a deeply notched tail.

short, conical bill

brown-streaked back

bright red eyebrow, forecrown, throat and breast

♂

heavily streaked flanks

♀

square tail

Nesting: in a cavity, building, dense foliage or abandoned bird nest; open cup nest of plants and other debris; pale blue, spotted eggs are ¾ x ⁹⁄₁₆ in; female incubates 4–5 eggs for 12–14 days.

Did You Know?

The variation in the male House Finch's plumage, which ranges from light yellow-orange to bright red, is thought to be the result of diet. Females choose the reddest males with which to breed.

American Goldfinch
Carduelis tristis

Like vibrant rays of sunshine, American Goldfinches cheerily flutter about in spring and summer. It is hard to miss their jubilant *po-ta-to-chip* call and their distinctive, undulating flight style. • Because these acrobatic birds regularly feed while hanging upside down, finch feeders are designed with the seed-openings below the perches. These feeders discourage the more aggressive House Sparrows, which feed upright, from stealing the seeds. Use niger or black-oil sunflower seeds to attract American Goldfinches to your bird feeder.

Other ID: *Nonbreeding male:* olive brown back; yellow-tinged head; gray underparts; dark wings with broad wing bars, dark bill. *Breeding female:* yellow throat and breast; yellow-green belly; pinkish bill. *Nonbreeding female:* grayish overall.
Size: L 4½–5 in; W 9 in.
Voice: song is a long, varied series of trills, twitters, warbles and hissing notes; calls include *po-ta-to-chip* or *per-chic-or-ee* (often delivered in flight) and a whistled *dear-me, see-me.*
Status: common permanent resident; numbers are augmented in migration and winter.
Habitat: weedy fields, woodland edges, meadows, riparian areas, parks and gardens.

Similar Birds

Evening Grosbeak   Wilson's Warbler

yellow-green
upparts

black cap
extends onto
forehead

black wings
with white
wing bars

♀

orange bill

♂

white rump
and undertail
coverts

orange legs

breeding

Nesting: in the fork of a deciduous tree; compact cup nest of plant fibers, grass and spider silk; pale bluish eggs are ⅝ x ½ in; female incubates 4–6 eggs for 12–14 days.

Did You Know?

These birds nest in late summer to ensure that there is a dependable source of seeds to feed their young.

Look For

American Goldfinches delight in perching on late-summer thistle heads or poking through dandelion patches in search of seeds.

House Sparrow

Passer domesticus

A black mask and "bib" adorn the male of this adaptive, aggressive species. The House Sparrow's tendency to usurp territory has led to a decline in some native bird populations. This species will even help itself to another bird's home, such as a bluebird box or a Purple Martin house. Recently, however, populations of this "weaver finch" (this bird is not a true sparrow) have actually declined here as well. • House Sparrows have a high reproductive output. A pair may raise up to four clutches per year, with up to eight young per clutch.

Other ID: *Breeding male:* gray crown; dark bill; dark, mottled upperparts; white wing bar. *Nonbreeding male:* pale bill; smaller black "bib" *Female:* indistinct facial patterns; plain gray-brown overall; streaked upperparts; grayish, unstreaked underparts.
Size: L 5½–6½ in; W 9½ in.
Voice: song is a plain, familiar *cheep-cheep-cheep-cheep;* call is a short *chill-up.*
Status: common permanent resident.
Habitat: townsites, urban and suburban areas, backyard feeders, farmyards and agricultural areas, railway yards and other developed areas.

Similar Birds

Dickcissel

Look For

In spring, House Sparrows feast on the buds of fruit trees and will sometimes eat lettuce from backyard gardens

buffy eyebrow

chestnut nape

black lore and "bib"

light gray cheek

♀

grayish, unstreaked underparts

♂

breeding

Nesting: often communal; in a birdhouse, under eaves or behind window shutters, in an ornamental shrub or natural cavity; pair builds a large dome nest of grass, twigs and plant fibers; gray-speckled, white to greenish eggs are ⅞ x ⅝ in; pair incubates 4–6 eggs for 10–13 days.

Did You Know?

This conspicuous bird was introduced to North America from Europe in the 1850s as part of a plan to control insects. As it turns out, these birds are largely vegetarian!

Glossary

brood: *n.* a family of young from one hatching; v. to sit on eggs so as to hatch them.

buteo: a high-soaring hawk (genus *Buteo*); characterized by broad wings and short, wide tails; feeds mostly on small mammals and other land animals.

cere: a fleshy area at the base of a bird's bill that contains the nostrils.

clutch: the number of eggs laid by the female at one time.

corvid: a member of the crow family (Corvidae); includes crows, jays, ravens and magpies.

crop: an enlargement of the esophagus; serves as a storage structure and (in pigeons) has glands that produce secretions.

dabbling: a foraging technique used by ducks, in which the head and neck are submerged but the body and tail remain on the water's surface; dabbling ducks can usually walk easily on land, can take off without running and have brightly colored speculums.

eclipse plumage: a cryptic plumage, similar to that of females, worn by some male ducks in fall when they molt their flight feathers and consequently are unable to fly.

endangered: a species that is facing extirpation or extinction in all or part of its range.

extirpated: a species that no longer exists in the wild in a particular region but occurs elsewhere.

fledge: to leave the nest for the first time.

fledgling: a young bird that has left the nest but is dependent upon its parents.

flushing: a behavior in which frightened birds explode into flight in response to a disturbance.

flycatching: a feeding behavior in which the bird leaves a perch, snatches an insect in midair and returns to the same perch.

hawking: attempting to catch insects through aerial pursuit.

leading edge: the front edge of the wing as viewed from below.

mantle: feathers of the back and upperside of folded wings.

molt: the periodic shedding and regrowth of worn feathers (often twice per year).

morph: one of several alternate plumages displayed by members of a species.

primaries: the outermost flight feathers.

riparian: refers to habitat along riverbanks.

rufous: rusty red in color.

speculum: a brightly colored patch on the wings of many dabbling ducks.

vagrant: a transient bird found outside its normal range.

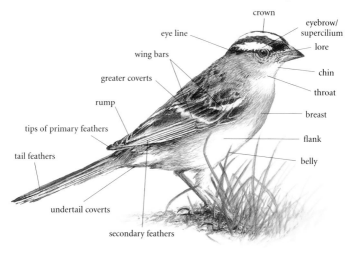

Checklist

The following checklist contains 322 species of birds that have been officially recorded in New Jersey. Species are grouped by family and listed in taxonomic order in accordance with the A.O.U. *Check-list of North American Birds* (7th ed.) and its supplements.

Accidental and casual species (those that are not seen on a yearly basis) are listed in *italics*. In addition, the following risk categories are also noted: endangered (en), threatened (th) and special concern (sc).

We wish to thank the New Jersey Audubon Society for providing the information for this checklist.

Waterfowl
❑ Greater White-Fronted Goose
❑ Snow Goose
❑ *Ross's Goose*
❑ Brant
❑ Cackling Goose
❑ Canada Goose
❑ Mute Swan
❑ Tundra Swan
❑ Wood Duck
❑ Gadwall
❑ Eurasian Wigeon
❑ American Wigeon
❑ American Black Duck
❑ Mallard
❑ Blue-winged Teal
❑ Northern Shoveler
❑ Northern Pintail
❑ Green-winged Teal
❑ Canvasback
❑ Redhead
❑ Ring-necked Duck
❑ Greater Scaup
❑ Lesser Scaup
❑ King Eider
❑ Common Eider
❑ Harlequin Duck
❑ Surf Scoter
❑ White-winged Scoter
❑ Black Scoter
❑ Long-tailed Duck
❑ Bufflehead
❑ Common Goldeneye
❑ Hooded Merganser (th)
❑ Common Merganser
❑ Red-breasted Merganser
❑ Ruddy Duck

Grouse & Allies
❑ Ring-necked Pheasant
❑ Ruffed Grouse
❑ Wild Turkey

New World Quail
❑ Northern Bobwhite

Loons
❑ Red-throated Loon
❑ Common Loon

Grebes
❑ Pied-billed Grebe (en)
❑ Horned Grebe
❑ Red-necked Grebe

Petrels & Shearwaters
❑ Northern Fulmar

❑ Cory's Shearwater
❑ Greater Shearwater
❑ Sooty Shearwater
❑ Manx Shearwater
❑ Audubon's Shearwater

Storm-Petrels
❑ Wilson's Storm-Petrel

Gannets
❑ Northern Gannet

Pelicans
❑ American White Pelican
❑ Brown Pelican

Cormorants
❑ Double-crested Cormorant
❑ Great Cormorant

Herons
❑ American Bittern (en)
❑ Least Bittern (sc)
❑ Great Blue Heron (sc)
❑ Great Egret
❑ Snowy Egret
❑ Little Blue Heron
❑ Tricolored Heron
❑ Cattle Egret
❑ Green Heron
❑ Black-crowned
   Night-Heron (th)
❑ Yellow-crowned
   Night-Heron (th)

Ibises
❑ Glossy Ibis

Vultures
❑ Black Vulture
❑ Turkey Vulture

Kites, Hawks & Eagles
❑ Osprey (th)
❑ Swallow-tailed Kite
❑ Mississippi Kite
❑ Bald Eagle (en)
❑ Northern Harrier (en)
❑ Sharp-shinned Hawk (sc)

❑ Cooper's Hawk (th)
❑ Northern Goshawk (en)
❑ Red-shouldered Hawk (en)
❑ Broad-winged Hawk (sc)
❑ Red-tailed Hawk
❑ Rough-legged Hawk
❑ Golden Eagle

Falcons
❑ American Kestrel (sc)
❑ Merlin
❑ Peregrine Falcon (en)

Rails, Gallinules & Coots
❑ Black Rail (th)
❑ Clapper Rail
❑ King Rail (sc)
❑ Virginia Rail
❑ Sora
❑ Common Moorhen
❑ American Coot

Cranes
❑ Sandhill Crane

Plovers
❑ Black-bellied Plover
❑ American Golden-Plover
❑ Semipalmated Plover
❑ Piping Plover (en)
❑ Killdeer

Oystercatchers
❑ American Oystercatcher

Stilts & Avocets
❑ Black-necked Stilt
❑ American Avocet

Sandpipers & Allies
❑ Greater Yellowlegs
❑ Lesser Yellowlegs
❑ Solitary Sandpiper
❑ Willet
❑ Spotted Sandpiper (sc)
❑ Upland Sandpiper (en)
❑ Whimbrel
❑ Hudsonian Godwit
❑ Marbled Godwit

❏ Ruddy Turnstone
❏ Red Knot (th)
❏ Sanderling (sc)
❏ Semipalmated Sandpiper
❏ Western Sandpiper
❏ Least Sandpiper
❏ White-rumped Sandpiper
❏ Baird's Sandpiper
❏ Pectoral Sandpiper
❏ Purple Sandpiper
❏ Dunlin
❏ Stilt Sandpiper
❏ Buff-breasted Sandpiper
❏ Ruff
❏ Short-billed Dowitcher
❏ Long-billed Dowitcher
❏ Wilson's Snipe
❏ American Woodcock
❏ Wilson's Phalarope
❏ Red-necked Phalarope
❏ Red Phalarope

Gulls & Allies
❏ Pomarine Jaeger
❏ Parasitic Jaeger
❏ Long-tailed Jaeger
❏ Laughing Gull
❏ Little Gull
❏ Black-headed Gull
❏ Bonaparte's Gull
❏ Ring-billed Gull
❏ Herring Gull
❏ Iceland Gull
❏ Lesser Black-backed Gull
❏ Glaucous Gull
❏ Great Black-backed Gull
❏ Black-legged Kittiwake
❏ Gull-billed Tern
❏ Caspian Tern (sc)
❏ Royal Tern
❏ Common Tern (sc)
❏ Forster's Tern
❏ Least Tern (en)
❏ Black Tern (sc)

Skimmers
❏ Black Skimmer

Alcids
❏ Dovekie
❏ Razorbill
❏ Atlantic Puffin

Pigeons & Doves
❏ Rock Pigeon
❏ Mourning Dove

Cuckoos
❏ Black-billed Cuckoo
❏ Yellow-billed Cuckoo

Barn Owls
❏ Barn Owl (sc)

Owls
❏ Eastern Screech-Owl
❏ Great Horned Owl
❏ Snowy Owl
❏ Barred Owl (th)
❏ Long-eared Owl (th)
❏ Short-eared Owl (en)
❏ Northern Saw-whet Owl

Nightjars
❏ Common Nighthawk (sc)
❏ Chuck-will's-widow
❏ Whip-poor-will

Swifts
❏ Chimney Swift

Hummingbirds
❏ Ruby-throated Hummingbird

Kingfishers
❏ Belted Kingfisher

Woodpeckers
❏ Red-headed Woodpecker
❏ Red-bellied Woodpecker
❏ Yellow-bellied Sapsucker
❏ Downy Woodpecker
❏ Hairy Woodpecker
❏ Northern Flicker
❏ Pileated Woodpecker

Flycatchers
❏ Olive-sided Flycatcher
❏ Eastern Wood-Pewee
❏ Yellow-bellied Flycatcher

❏ Acadian Flycatcher
❏ Alder Flycatcher
❏ Willow Flycatcher
❏ Least Flycatcher (sc)
❏ Eastern Phoebe
❏ Great Crested Flycatcher
❏ Western Kingbird
❏ Eastern Kingbird

Shrikes
❏ Northern Shrike

Vireos
❏ White-eyed Vireo
❏ Yellow-throated Vireo
❏ Blue-headed Vireo (sc)
❏ Warbling Vireo
❏ Philadelphia Vireo
❏ Red-eyed Vireo

Jays & Crows
❏ Blue Jay
❏ American Crow
❏ Fish Crow
❏ Common Raven

Larks
❏ Horned Lark (sc)

Swallows
❏ Purple Martin
❏ Tree Swallow
❏ Northern Rough-winged
   Swallow
❏ Bank Swallow
❏ Cliff Swallow (sc)
❏ Barn Swallow

Chickadees & Titmice
❏ Carolina Chickadee
❏ Black-capped Chickadee
❏ *Boreal Chickadee*
❏ Tufted Titmouse

Nuthatches
❏ Red-breasted Nuthatch
❏ White-breasted Nuthatch

Creepers
❏ Brown Creeper

Wrens
❏ Carolina Wren
❏ House Wren
❏ Winter Wren (sc)
❏ Sedge Wren (en)
❏ Marsh Wren

Kinglets
❏ Golden-crowned Kinglet
❏ Ruby-crowned Kinglet

Gnatcatchers
❏ Blue-gray Gnatcatcher

Thrushes
❏ Eastern Bluebird
❏ Veery (sc)
❏ Gray-cheeked Thrush (sc)
❏ Bicknell's Thrush
❏ Swainson's Thrush
❏ Hermit Thrush
❏ Wood Thrush
❏ American Robin

Mockingbirds & Thrashers
❏ Gray Catbird
❏ Northern Mockingbird
❏ Brown Thrasher

Starlings
❏ European Starling

Wagtails & Pipits
❏ American Pipit

Waxwings
❏ Cedar Waxwing

Wood-Warblers
❏ Blue-winged Warbler
❏ Golden-winged Warbler (sc)
❏ Tennessee Warbler
❏ Orange-crowned Warbler
❏ Nashville Warbler
❏ Northern Parula (sc)
❏ Yellow Warbler
❏ Chestnut-sided Warbler
❏ Magnolia Warbler
❏ Cape May Warbler
❏ Black-throated Blue Warbler

❏ Yellow-rumped Warbler
❏ Black-throated Green
  Warbler (sc)
❏ Blackburnian Warbler (th)
❏ Yellow-throated Warbler
❏ Pine Warbler
❏ Prairie Warbler
❏ Palm Warbler
❏ Bay-breasted Warbler
❏ Blackpoll Warbler
❏ Cerulean Warbler (sc)
❏ Black-and-white Warbler
❏ American Redstart
❏ Prothonotary Warbler
❏ Worm-eating Warbler
❏ Ovenbird
❏ Northern Waterthrush
❏ Louisiana Waterthrush
❏ Kentucky Warbler (sc)
❏ Connecticut Warbler
❏ Mourning Warbler
❏ Common Yellowthroat
❏ Hooded Warbler
❏ Wilson's Warbler
❏ Canada Warbler (sc)
❏ Yellow-breasted Chat (sc)

Tanagers
❏ Summer Tanager
❏ Scarlet Tanager

Sparrows & Allies
❏ Eastern Towhee
❏ American Tree Sparrow
❏ Chipping Sparrow
❏ Field Sparrow
❏ Vesper Sparrow (en)
❏ *Lark Sparrow*
❏ Savannah Sparrow (th)
❏ Grasshopper Sparrow (th)
❏ Nelson's Sharp-tailed
  Sparrow
❏ Saltmarsh Sharp-tailed
  Sparrow
❏ Seaside Sparrow

❏ Fox Sparrow
❏ Song Sparrow
❏ Lincoln's Sparrow
❏ Swamp Sparrow
❏ White-throated Sparrow
❏ White-crowned Sparrow
❏ Dark-eyed Junco
❏ Lapland Longspur
❏ Snow Bunting

Grosbeaks & Buntings
❏ Northern Cardinal
❏ Rose-breasted Grosbeak
❏ Blue Grosbeak
❏ Indigo Bunting
❏ Dickcissel

Blackbirds & Allies
❏ Bobolink (th)
❏ Red-winged Blackbird
❏ Eastern Meadowlark (sc)
❏ Rusty Blackbird
❏ Common Grackle
❏ Boat-tailed Grackle
❏ Brown-headed Cowbird
❏ Orchard Oriole
❏ Baltimore Oriole

Finches
❏ Purple Finch
❏ House Finch
❏ *Red Crossbill*
❏ *White-winged Crossbill*
❏ *Common Redpoll*
❏ Pine Siskin
❏ American Goldfinch
❏ Evening Grosbeak

Old World Sparrows
❏ House Sparrow

Select References

Baicich, Paul J. and C.J.O. Harrison. 1997. *A Guide to the Nests, Eggs and Nestlings of North American Birds.* 2nd ed. Natural World Academic Press, San Diego, CA.

Boyle, William Jr. 2002. *A Guide to Bird Finding in New Jersey.* Rutger's University Press, New Brunswick, NJ.

Ehrlich, Paul R., David Dobkin and Darryl Wheye. 1988. *The Birder's Handbook: A Field Guide to the Natural History of North American Birds.* Simon and Schuster, New York.

Kaufman, Kenn. 1996. *Lives of North American Birds.* Houghton Mifflin, New York.

Roth, Sally. 1998. *Attracting Birds to Your Backyard.* Rodale Press, Emmaus, PA.

Schneck, Marcus. 1999. *Garden Bird Facts.* Quantum Books, London, England.

Sibley, David Allen. 2003. *The Sibley Field Guide to Birds of Eastern North America.* Alfred A. Knopf, New York.

Sibley, David Allen. 2001. *The Sibley Guide to Birds.* Alfred A. Knopf, New York.

Sibley, David Allen. 1997. *The Birds of Cape May.* 2nd ed. New Jersey Audubon Society, Bernardsville, NJ.

Walsh, Joan, Vince Elia, Rich Kane and Thomas Halliwell. 1999. *Birds of New Jersey.* New Jersey Audubon Society, Bernardsville, NJ.

Index

Boat-tailed Grackle